I left work right at 5 and hurried to the church where I was to meet my friends. They were going to celebrate with me the awesome occasion of my thirtieth birthday.

The minister of the church, who happened to be chatting with the group, looked up as I entered. He broke off his conversation with others in the group, gave me a big smile, and stuck his left arm straight out with the thumb pointing toward the floor. "Your chances just went down like that!" he said, still smiling.

I was shocked that anyone could be so cruel. Then we all laughed nervously as I joked about my over-the-hill status and the lonely spinsterhood I now faced.

Are you single, or about to be single again?

How do you handle the pressures of belonging to a minority in a society that frequently views singles as second-class citizens?

Do you try to defend your status, or do you accept the pigeonhole you've been put into?

How do you relate to your church?

Perhaps more important, how do you handle the internal pressures of identity, self-image, wayward sexual desires, finances, and perhaps having to be both mother and father to children?

Bob and I have lived with these questions. We would like to share what we have found with you.

JESUS WAS A SINGLE ADULT

BOB & JUNE VETTER

David C. Cook Publishing Co.

ELGIN, ILLINOIS—WESTON, ONTARIO

Edited by Sharrel Keyes
Cover design by Kurt Dietsch
Printed in the United States of America

ISBN 0-89191-109-X
LC 77-88655

To the many single people
who have enriched our lives.

CONTENTS

PROLOGUE
(Bob)

EVERYTHING IN THE ROOM was dark, and the two of us were fast asleep. The telephone on the floor jangled like the first ring of an alarm clock.

I ran my hand across the rug until my groping fingers hit the phone. I lifted the receiver, and the small light on the dial lit up.

"Bob? This is Susan. I hope I didn't wake you, but I just needed to talk to someone."

I rested my head back on the pillow and made agreeing grunts to assure Susan I was indeed awake. For the next forty-five minutes I heard a typical story. This mother of three children had just come back from her psychologist's group meeting and needed more answers. Her husband was not

going to support her and their children in the way the separation agreement stated; the lawyers on both sides were not
doing anything to resolve her dilemma; she needed money
but was afraid to work because her attorney told her it would
hurt her support case in the final settlement . . . and so on into
the depths of another person badly crushed by her new state
of singleness.

Another night . . . another call. June, my wife, answers this
time. A single woman has been taken advantage of by her
supervisor at work. On many occasions he has made lewd
remarks and offered numerous propositions. Today she
complained to his superior, only to get a smile, a shrug of the
shoulders. She was single and attractive, he said. What did
she expect?

Where are you at this moment? Standing in a bookshop?
Waiting for a train? Seated alone in your apartment late at
night wrestling with your problems?

You must be single, or planning to be, or perhaps you are
interested in the person of Jesus Christ—otherwise our title
would not have attracted you. Who are you, anyway?

During the past few years, you and the rest of society have
become intrigued about your status in life. There are singles'
weekends, singles' bars, singles' dances, singles' magazines,
and organizations for single parents. You are an enigma
because of this word *single,* and you are as fascinated about
yourself as the world is fascinated by you.

If you stand alone by choice, others wonder why. If you are
alone because of the death of your mate, you are respectfully
accepted but relegated to the set-apart role called "widow."
If you are alone as a result of divorce, you are suspect, a
threat, an easy mark, or a pitiful failure.

This book is for you and about you. It is written by a married couple who knows where you are because we each have recently been there. I was a widower at age thirty-five with three children to raise. I found the reentry into single life a terrifying experience. All of a sudden I was in a different world: relationships with my friends changed; I didn't have the same base from which to make decisions. Life was no longer as comfortable, as secure, as "normal."

June was single for thirty-three years before we married; she had to face questions of self-worth, career choices, and family responsibilities.

Our feet have scuffed in the dust of the single life, and we find that some of it has remained on our skin. As soloists in this society, we laughed your laughs, cried your tears, and grieved in your emptiness. We rode the merry-go-round of words and lights that invite "singles" to a life of never-ending fun. But we found somehow the music was never quite in tune and the golden ring was always unreachable.

In the following chapters, we will relate some of our own experiences and those of other singles we have known through the Christian Singles Foundation, a ministry in the New England states that assists the formerly married single to adjust to his or her new role. We will try to help with some of the practical issues involved in being single: how to handle finances, problems of sex, love, and loneliness.

Jesus was a single young adult. He neither defended his role nor gloried in it. He was a whole man who was also single; his marital status neither made him nor broke him. He knew what it was to care for an elderly parent, to be a single guest in others' homes, to be on the move constantly. And he knew what it was to be stared at and watched.

If you are standing up, we invite you to sit down somewhere and follow us through these pages. We hope to give you some insights into yourself and a new outlook on your single life.

THE
PAST

ONE
SINGLE AGAIN
(Bob)

I KEPT THE RECEIVER pressed to my ear as the telephone rang and rang. I had been waiting all day for some good news from the doctor, and finally the familiar voice answered.

"I'm returning your call," I said. "Is there any definite word?"

After a moment of eternal silence the doctor said, "We lost her."

Not sure of the message, I asked him to repeat it.

"We lost her. I'm sorry, but we lost her."

My first reaction was, "How can they lose a patient in a major hospital? They probably put her in the wrong room!" Then, as if I had been hit with a direct right to the jaw, I understood. My wife was dead.

That moment of unbelief, terror, hate, anger, self-pity, love, and frustration seemed eternal. What do I do? What about the children? Why did she die? I loved her too much to let her die! Where did I go wrong?

This is the trauma of separation—separation by death, a final, irreversible act that destroys both parties of the love relationship.

Some of you reading this book have been on a similar telephone, or at a bedside, or in the hospital waiting room, and you know the helplessness and the finality of that moment.

Perhaps your single status is not a result of the death of a loved one but of the death of a marriage instead. Divorce or legal separation can be even more painful than separation by death.

June and I know a woman who looked in her husband's briefcase for the plane tickets he had promised to pick up for their vacation, only to find a torrid love letter he had written to another woman. She read about how she, his wife, had grown stale and how his lover was now the spark of his life.

It sounds like a soap opera, but it isn't. It is the true story of the death of a marriage. To place five, ten, or twenty years of trust in a person, and then have it murdered in one act before your eyes, is as if one of your children were being crushed under the wheels of a giant truck and you could do nothing but stand helplessly and watch.

Our thoughts about the single life come in large part from the painful experiences of persons who have lost a husband or wife as a result of death, divorce, or separation. We will turn to the experiences of friends who have been through the trauma of divorce. Here, I want to deal with singleness from my own experience of being a widower.

As I look back over the days I spent attending college, falling in love, getting married, finding a career, and becoming a father, I realize that I did what came most naturally and what I had been taught was right for every young man or woman to do.

I always believed I would one day wed, settle down with a wife and family, and live happily ever after. My friends had the same goals and expectations; we were conditioned to be married. Only in the past few years have people started looking at singleness as a valid option.

I found in the death of my wife not only a deep personal loss, but a total revolution in the life-style for which I was groomed and into which I had fit very well.

Death is always a blow to the person who is left. I experienced the very sudden loss of my wife with less than a day's warning that she was severely ill. Others have experienced death as a long, slow process. Although some have time to prepare for the death of their marriage partner, they almost never take time or desire to think of being a single person again.

But no matter what the circumstances, we have all had to wake up one morning and say, "Oh, God, tell me it is not true that I am alone."

I can remember being alone during the first days after my wife's death. Those days were filled with people, things to do, legal matters to care for, and going through the motions of earning a living. Those were not the real lonely days. I woke up knowing that today would be full of friends, activity, errands to run, all of which would keep me company and not let me hide in my fears.

But one morning I woke up early. The sun was struggling to cast its first rays between the morning clouds. I began to think, *What will I do today?* There was no answer. I was alone. My plans were gone. I had no desire to attempt a new venture. The world around me was a dull, endless gray. At that moment I was hit by the true impact of being all alone, single again.

I rolled over in my large, vacant bed and looked at the

pillow that once held the head of the one I loved. Now it was wrinkle-free and vacant. The sheets were cold, almost damp. Every glance of that gray morning bore the same message. *I'm alone. Single again.*

For me, as for many others in similar situations, it meant being single for the first time in my adult life. .

A friend of mine, who had lost his wife a few years before, had given me some very hard advice. He said, "Bob, one day the reality of your wife's death and your being alone is going to hit you like a truck." He went on, "It may not come for six months or a year. But be sure of one thing. It *will* come hard." As I lay in that bed on that gray morning, those words came back to me. I had just been "hit."

If you have gone through a divorce, that gray day comes just as hard and perhaps more viciously to you. Very few divorces are so clean that two people can walk away from each other without experiencing grief. In many instances, they not only feel grief but hate as well. The gray day for the divorced not only comes with the reality of being alone but with the reality of having been rejected, humiliated, cheated, and in most cases, violated. Surviving these days is most difficult, but when they pass, the impact of being single in a married society becomes a daily revelation with which to cope.

Not only does the impact of living in a married society come forcefully, but the everyday routines that were once done without thinking can be overwhelming. The September after my wife died, I went to Sears to buy some dungarees and sneakers for the boys. I was standing in the clothing department wrestling through the stacks of pants, totally frustrated by my ignorance of sizes. The housewives buzzing around me suddenly became too much. I had to put the articles down on the counter and just walk out of the store in order to regain my composure.

For some it is not the dungarees shopping but some other

ordinary routine that will grow out of proportion. We know of several women who found that their once-lovely home, the token of all their affections and efforts, had become their hell. Some of you know what it is like to listen to a bathroom faucet drip for two or three weeks because you do not know how to repair it or you cannot afford calling a plumber. The dripping faucet soon becomes a pounding in the middle of the night, booming louder and louder until it is almost like cannon volleys as you lay helpless in your emotional prison.

Whether you are a widow, widower, or divorced person, one new experience that will most likely cause you much emotional pain is the role of being both father and mother to your children. The divorced sometimes think that the other partner will still be around to fulfill her or his role. We have found that in many cases this is not true. Once the partner who seeks the divorce or who causes the ultimate separation is gone from the home, his or her feeling of responsibility for those children decreases drastically.

The new mother/father role is a difficult one. Disaster can strike at any time, especially when you least expect it. You are on your way to work, ready to go out the front door, when one of the children says, "I don't have any socks to wear to school today, Daddy." I am sure you know all the lines that follow!

"If you didn't kick them under your bed, they would be in the wash . . . . What do you do with them, eat them every week? . . . Don't be ridiculous, I did ten pairs on Saturday!"

Soon the smiles turn to tears, both the child's and yours. Now you are late for work, you are angry at the child, you are angry with yourself for getting angry with your child, and the child is upset. All over a silly pair of socks. Emotionally, it gets to be too much.

But I do need to mention that one of the greatest surprises for me, and for others with whom I have talked, is the lack of support the formerly married single receives from the body of believers once the grief period is over.

In my own personal situation the support I received from my Christian friends in and out of the local church was tremendous during the grief period. My children and I were supported by so many people's actions and prayers during those difficult days. What I discovered some sixty days later, though, was that I had become an official member of the single society, and it became more and more difficult for most Christian friends to include me in their "couples" thinking. This was true for me as a widower, but it is much more true for the divorced.

One of the women in our Christian singles group told me once, "I would have been better off to kill my husband than to let him divorce me. The church can forgive a murderer much faster than it can forgive a divorcee." The more I think about that statement, the more I begin to realize the truth in it.

We have found in the last two years that this attitude is beginning to change. Slowly, very slowly, the church is beginning to see the needs of the formerly married. One pastor invited us to talk with a group in his church about the needs they faced as widowed and divorced singles, and afterwards he said to us, "I have been in the ministry for more than twenty-five years, and I have never heard such openness and such hurt in all my life. I never realized so many people were hurting this way and that the church was failing to relate to the needs of these dear people." His church has now begun a singles ministry.

This past summer we visited England for a week. During our stay, we drove some seven hundred miles through the countryside. My first experience with driving on the left-hand side of the road was terror. I would like to push this illustration a bit by likening it to being single in today's society.

For the formerly married person in the church, it is like arriving at an airport and being met by a state policeman who issues a proclamation that, because you are single, you must continue to drive on the left-hand side of the road in the United States. After being in England for a week you might think, *I can handle this now with several hundred miles of left-side driving under my belt.* But when everyone else is continuing to drive on the right, terror sets in.

As a formerly married single, you come seeking love and shelter in the church. But much to our dismay, that spiritual rest stop is filled with snipers and traps.

What is the result of such an experience? Many singles simply get off the highway of Christian growth and never travel it again. Others very quietly drive in the breakdown lane, sitting in the back of the church, coming in and out quietly, hoping no one will hit them head-on.

Some will read this and say we are exaggerating. But we know person after person who went to the church to find acceptance and help after being divorced, only to be driven out by ridicule, and the pointing finger of judgment. One young woman said, "It is like having the word *divorced* branded in your forehead. I felt like a leper."

In defense of the church, we must remember that it is basically a marriage institution. The Bible includes such statements as, "It is not good for the man to live alone" (Gen. 2: 18) and, "It is better to marry than to burn with passion" (1 Cor. 7: 9). Unfortunately, the church reads the next few verses of 1 Corinthians 7 about divorce and remarrying and then forgets all the teaching on love, forgiveness, acceptance, and the charge not to judge. It often throws out the formerly married, never stopping to realize how many hurts and wounds they have and how much they need the healing balm of Christ.

By writing this we are not trying to embarrass the church. Our cry is to warn you, as a formerly married single, to fasten your seat belt and to realize there could be a rough road ahead for you in the church. You may get hit broadside when you least expect it.

Our cry is also to the church. We plead with the church to reach out in love to the single and to accept the formerly married person. We are not defending divorce. Rather, we are saying that divorce is here, and it is affecting Christian marriages as well as non-Christian marriages. We must take a strong stand on *love* and realize that we need to show Christ's love to people immersed in this problem. Formerly married Christian singles need Christ's healing and the love that only he can give. We must not prevent them from receiving that love because of our own bias.

Every time I hear of a single or formerly married person being put down by Mr. Spirituality, I think of the words of Christ on the cross, "Forgive them, Father! They don't know what they are doing" (Luke 23: 34). To the single I can only say, Jesus loves and cares, for he, too, was single and rejected.

TWO
LEAVING THE PAST BEHIND
(June)

MARILYN, A TALL, BLONDE, young woman, sat rigidly on the corner of the sofa. I could not help but notice her stiffness from across the room. It was in marked contrast to the laughter, easy movement, and conversation of others as they talked in the living room and den during the refreshment time that followed our singles' meeting.

My hostess role made it easy for me to approach Marilyn and invite her into the dining room for cookies. She smiled and moved by my side into the other room. We made our selections and returned to the living room, where Marilyn sat once again on the corner of the sofa. As her conversation became more free, I learned this was her first social gathering since her divorce was granted six months before.

"Friends of mine told me about this group before they moved away," she told me. "I haven't gone to anything other than Karl and Angie's house since my separation, but now they've moved to New York. They told me to come here and meet other people who have gone through what I have."

Through a mutual friend of ours, Karl and Angie had heard about Christian Singles and the monthly meetings at our house. Angie had called once, asking if we would mind her bringing Marilyn to one of the meetings to help her through the discomfort of so many new people to meet. We had encouraged her to come, but plans fell through. Now Angie had moved, and Marilyn had found the courage to come on her own.

She and I spent the whole evening together. I never left her side, although we did leave the sofa and move around. As we passed friends who had been coming to the meetings for some months, I introduced Marilyn. After that evening, Bob and I invited her and her daughters back to the house for dessert one Sunday afternoon, and we encouraged a close friend in the group, one who had worked out her postdivorce grief and readjustments fairly well, to contact her. Charlotte did this, and within a few weeks both women were enjoying their new friendship. Charlotte was able to share with Marilyn her own readjustment process, and Marilyn felt free to air her hurts and feelings as they arose.

The key to being able to move ahead and begin again after the death of a partner or marriage is to be able to *leave the past behind.*

Those four words are easy to write, even easier to utter, but to *practice* leaving the past behind is difficult. It takes energy, determination, concentrated effort, and friends to help.

A man in his late forties told us recently as he struggled with this same issue, "I find it so hard to let go. My wife has started her new life, the kids have gotten over the shock and are adjusting now, but I still am angry, hurt, and bitter. I know I have to force myself to start doing things and going places, but it is so hard."

24

Charlotte later told us of her own experience. "I had to examine all the things that made my new role as a single person difficult. As I took these things one by one, I was better able to deal with them. For instance, my whole sense of security as a married woman was in knowing that at the end of the day my husband would come home. When I was single again, knowing that someone was *not* coming home really bothered me and made me feel unsettled. But when I thought more about it, I realized how much I had been alone when I was married. My husband and I didn't do all that much together. I began to realize that things were not so different now that he was gone.

"The same thing was true in decision making. When I realized I was responsible for making all the decisions about my life, my house, my children, it scared me. Again, as I thought it out, I began to see that when I was married, my husband had been away from the family a lot, and I had been making these kinds of decision on my own for quite some time. As these truths became apparent to me, it helped me realize that everything in my new life was not as foreign as I once thought it would be."

Spiritually, she had become angry with God for allowing this crisis to take place in her life until, she says, "I realized I had not given much thought to God for a good many years."

Perhaps the most difficult part of putting the past behind is to overcome the anger, bitterness, hurt, and sense of failure that characterizes a divorce situation. These emotions become instant reruns in our mind's eye as we recount the tragedy suddenly surrounding our whole existence. Our ego is deflated, our self-image defaced, and our hope is gone.

FIRST STEPS

What positive steps can we take to build a new life? One statement by our friend Charlotte sticks in my mind. "Build on the good parts of your marriage." She reminded us that it is easier to recall the hurt than any happiness that existed, but happiness in most instances *did* exist at one time. "Those are the times to remember," she said.

One of the four psychological needs each of us possesses is the need for new experiences. (The other three are security, recognition, and freedom from guilt). To try something new is often very threatening, but it is also necessary. Few things will give as much satisfaction and confidence as trying, and succeeding, at something totally new.

For many women who find themselves divorced after years of marriage, this new experience comes when they return to the workforce. Often they need to take advantage of refresher courses in a local adult education center or college. The new routine and disciplines can be exhausting at first, but along with the exhaustion will come a confidence and satisfaction that is so vital to life.

Those who have small children and are unable to work full-time or return to school need to find other kinds of outlets, such as part-time employment or schooling, a new hobby or interest (a lifesaving or home repair course), or volunteer work. The best activities are those that bring you in contact with new people.

Leaving the past behind also means changing some things about your own person. If you have needed to start a diet for the past three years, now is the time to start counting calories. If you have wanted to cut your hair—or to let it grow—decide to do it now. Use the charts on pages 29-30.

Take the time to find out who you really are, what you really like, and what you can be as God's child. *Nothing* is as exciting as starting a new journey with him. Investigate the Scriptures as if you have never read them before. Look at Jesus as the person he was, unabashedly free in what he was called to do and how he was called to live, and let him lead you to a plateau you did not dream existed.

Another must for leaving the past behind is to find a friend or group of friends who will support you as you begin to move into your new life. These must be friends who will hold you accountable. For instance, if one of your new goals is to lose weight, they need to call you to task if you don't begin showing visible signs of staying on a diet. They should be able to make sure you do not slip back into, "Well, I couldn't pass that course anyway" type of thinking. They will be friends who will know your goals and pray with you as you work towards them, as well as help you evaluate your progress.

One of my favorite verses about Jesus is "He made up his mind and set out on his way to Jerusalem." In many instances we are told in Scripture how Christ avoided certain situations, saying, "My time has not yet come." But when it did come, he was ready to face it.

I believe the intensity of all Jesus was to suffer in the final days of his life was something he learned at the moment. Without question he knew he would be rejected, that he would suffer, that he would be killed. But did he know the magnitude of that suffering? I think not. He said, "Father, . . . if you will, take this cup of suffering away from me. Not my will, however, but your will be done." And we are told that, "In great anguish he prayed even more fervently; his sweat was like drops of blood falling to the ground" (Luke 22: 42, 44).

Would he get through the next hours with all they entailed? Yes. Did he *want* to go through them? Not if there was some other way. *Did* he go through them? Yes. And came out in glory on the other side!

Jesus "made up his mind and set out." Sometimes it is with this attitude that we need to move on to a new experience. Afraid? Yes. Hesitant? Perhaps. Looking for another way? Sometimes. But turning back? Never.

What has come into our lives is there sometimes by our own invitation, sometimes not. The question is, "What will I do now that I am in this place?"

JESUS WAS A SINGLE ADULT

Clinging to the past, or to what might have been, has never constructively helped a person live his/her life. Confronting the present, as it exists in reality, is the only way to move ahead. How are you doing in your battle to leave the past behind?

A Look at Life Now

What areas of my life that are basically out of my control have changed or must change as a result of death/divorce?

Living conditions   *Very Much*   *Moderate*   *Slight*
(Physical)

_____

Need to work

_____

Clubs/Organizations

_____

Church Affiliation

_____

Social activities

_____

Friends

_____

Do I feel overwhelmed
by   anger _____

      bitterness_____

      hurt _____

JESUS WAS A SINGLE ADULT

What specific areas of my life can I control to help me build a new life?

Friends who will pray with me/hold me accountable/share in a Bible study with me each week?

(List their names)

_____

_____

_____

Reading material to force me to think positively about myself and help me discover things about myself I didn't know. (At least one book a month for six months.)

_____

_____

_____

New hobby/interest/job within three months. List one school, one career counseling office and/or volunteer agency, one friend to visit in relation to this goal.

_____

_____

_____

What two things about myself would I like to change for a while? (Hairstyle? Amount of time watching TV? Weight? Reading habits?) What can I do today to start these changes?

_____

_____

_____

_____

THE
PRESENT

THREE

THE DEADLY WORLD OF FANTASY
(June)

IN ORDER TO LEAVE THE PAST BEHIND, some of us have to work hard at leaving the deadly world of fantasy behind.

Fantasizing is normal and healthy in young children. It is even beneficial in the teen years as young people dream about their acceptance by peers and the world at large and as they envision their future lives. But when fantasy becomes an escape, when it becomes preferred over the real world (which it often does for those who are alone), it is unhealthy, even lethal.

What's going on in a single adult's fantasy world? The formerly married find themselves dreaming about the "good old days" or "what I wish I would have done," while the never married often fantasize about the unexplored land of marriage and all its trimmings. Both groups can be plagued with the grass-is-greener disease, especially as they face the pressures of monotony or life in the present. And there are times when loneliness, or emotional lows, or biological urges team up with the imagination for our own private version of adult movies. We'll talk at greater length in a later chapter about how to deal with the common problem of sexual fantasies.

LIVING IN ANOTHER WORLD

When we fantasize, we are living in some other world, one in which we can manipulate people and events for our own ends. Or we are entering someone else's made-up world and agreeing to its terms as, for instance, when we become engrossed in a novel or a television drama.

What are some problems that accompany fantasizing? Let's look at the common example of picturing the type of person we hope to marry. Although we may not build up a physical description, we will probably romanticize and idealize our would-be partner in such a way that he/she could not possibly exist in anything as mundane as *human* life. When we do this, we keep ourselves from seeing the good, positive qualities in some of the single people around us. I've heard it said about a well-known bachelor in our area that God has not yet created the women who could meet his qualifications!

Sometimes our fantasies make it hard for us to discriminate between our desires concerning another person and what God actually has in store for us.

One young couple I know dated for two years. Both were committed Christians, both saw Christian service as their life goal, and both saw each other as the person God had picked out as their mate. Then one night at a prayer meeting, each of them felt God had revealed that the other person was *not* the individual to be his/her partner for life.

I think it is safe to say both individuals had one purpose: to serve God and to serve him completely. Because that was their ultimate heart-desire, I believe he made it clear in his own time, in his own way, about the relationship they had with one another.

Both later said how difficult it was for them to accept what God revealed to them that night and how hard the pull of parting was. Yet both (now married to other persons) look back with no doubts whatever that God made known his will at that prayer meeting in a way neither could deny.

Before I was married, there were two instances when I believed God was setting aside a certain person for me. The more I prayed about it, the more I was convinced that he indeed was speaking. But the relationships never developed that way.

Was I praying amiss? I don't believe so. One of the most beautiful verses I have found in Scripture during the last year is Ezekiel 36: 37: "I will once again let the Israelites ask me for help . . ." In other words, the Lord says to us, "Sure you can ask for this!" But having asked, we then need to take *his* answer and be satisfied with it.

When this verse first became meaningful to me, Bob and I were praying about a retreat center for singles, a refuge for those just coming through the death of a mate or the death of a marriage. It would be a place where people could receive informal or formal counseling, where there would be people to pray with, where help would be given in very practical matters such as learning how to budget money. There would be a place to go for a long walk or take a swim.

A friend of ours who is in real estate had shown us a beautiful piece of property overlooking the ocean. The layout of the house, the setting, everything seemed exactly what we needed as this harbor for those who suddenly found their lives shipwrecked.

I remember sharing the verse with friends at one of our singles' meetings and saying, "The Lord has said it is all right to ask for this. Now let's see if it is his will to give it to us."

It was not.

For six or eight months we prayed and prayed. The verse popped up again in my reading, and I was encouraged. I thought, "Yes, yes, the Lord is saying yes!"

We visited the house a second time, bringing friends with us who were also vitally concerned about a singles' center. Again we prayed. But the needed money did not materialize, and soon we heard that a developer had made an offer on the property, subject to the outcome of perk tests to assure that the facility could be turned into an apartment complex.

Within a short period of time we learned that, for a number of reasons, the property could not be approved as any type of multiple dwelling.

I had enquired . . . I had been heard . . . but the time and the setting were not God's plan.

So it is with our relationships from time to time. Our desires become so fervent; we set our eyes on a Christian marriage prospect, but somehow things don't turn out as we expected, and our spirits fall crushed.

A tendency among young women has often been to spend a lot of time wondering if a certain man is interested in them. This can lead to all kinds of fantasies. If he even looks in her direction, she wonders, *Did he notice me?* An older friend of mine—a woman with three married daughters of her own—once said to me, "Never sit around wondering if someone likes you and just doesn't know how to let you know. If he is interested, he'll find a way!

LIVING IN THE PAST

Fantasy for the formerly married person tends to be of the hindsight variety. Bob and I have known widows and widowers who have so romanticized the past that they are convinced nothing in the present or the future can ever compare with what once existed.

We once spent an afternoon with an attractive widow. We left her house saddened over her recent bereavement. It was a month or two later that we were told by another friend that this lady's husband had been dead for ten years. We were shocked. She had talked of their life together as if it were yesterday; her eyes glowed at every mention of her husband's name; and the tears welled up when she mentioned his death. Some time later she said to me, "I'm still standing at the casket, and I don't know how to walk away."

I knew a man who was widowed after only a few years of marriage. He was in his late twenties when his wife died. When he finally began to date—and for years afterwards—he often called his date by his wife's name. Twelve years after her death, he still carried the deceased woman's name on his checks and visited the home they had once shared together. It seemed impossible for him to break with the past. He lived in a world of fantasy.

The person who has been separated or divorced sometimes retreats into the fantasy world of what might have been . . . or should have been . . . or perhaps even will be again. "If only we had moved . . . if only I had been less selfish . . . if only we talked things out more . . . if only . . . ."

Another type of fantasy for the separated or divorced person revolves around anger, bitterness, and revenge. Which one of us has not mentally sought revenge against someone who has deeply hurt us? We calculate with every ounce of energy how we will retaliate when given the chance. But all the plotting and planning only drives us deeper into the pit of grief and unhappiness, while the life that could be turned around into something constructive passes by.

One person we know was so distraught over a divorce that he actually destroyed some property owned by his former mate. He agreed to pay for the damage he did, but he still broods on the cause of such irrational behavior.

LIVING IN YOUR NOW

Fantasy involves an attempt to escape. There is a cushion of safety that fantasy provides for the shattered heart, the crumbling ego, the fragile emotion. Things are safe in the controlled world of fantasy; in real life we are vulnerable and circumstances are not always in our control. It takes energy, determination, and the willingness to accept the pain of facing truth if we are to meet life head-on as it actually exists. On the other hand, it is so easy to retreat and hide. But there comes a time when almost all fantasizers find that pain infiltrates their hidden existence. Sooner or later they realize their fantasies are just that—a make-believe world that does not exist and never will. Somehow, for many, that pain is easier to tolerate than the reality of life as it actually surrounds them.

Our illustrations of fantasy could continue. You can make a television performer your closest friend; a man can take the centerfold model in *Playboy* as his sex partner. The list is endless. You can probably add your own.

You may ask, "Who does it hurt if I would rather live in a fantasy world in which I matter to someone and in which I get some degree of pleasure?" The answer is obvious: you hurt yourself. Because while you dream, the minutes and hours tick away, putting behind you time that can never be recaptured, time that can be used to bring out potential and accomplishments in you that you never believed were possible.

Conquering the fantasy dilemma is not easy, but it must be done if you are going to reach your true potential and are going to live an interesting and rewarding life. Some can do it alone; many others need professional counseling to deal with this problem. We do not pretend to be psychologists, but a few simple suggestions may help readers who find themselves in the fantasizer category.

The first step is to recognize that the world of fantasy is deadly and that you must leave it. The second step is to consciously watch yourself to learn *when* you drift into your make-believe world—while riding the subway to work? While waiting for your dinner to finish cooking? The third step is to divert your attention during those times to a constructive activity, such as reading a book while traveling, going out with someone to dinner, or inviting someone to come to your home.

As a starter, use the chart at the end of the chapter for one week. Fill in the appropriate time, place, and events that trigger you into your fantasy world. Carry it with you each day and whenever you find your mind wandering in these directions—while riding to work, watching television, or during your time of daydreaming—make a note of it.

Once you have obtained a general overview of your week and the times, places, and events that push you into your make-believe world, you will be better able to consciously mobilize your thoughts against this suffocating practice. During the second week, set short-term goals for using your mind in an active way to enrich your total being.

The main reason people fantasize is to find a place of acceptance and love. No one with a positive relationship with the real world needs to revert to the arena of make-believe. Those who do retreat into fantasy need to look again as their own self-image.

The person who has never married (especially those who have not particularly *chosen* to remain single) and the divorced or separated individual often suffer from a poor self-image. It is almost impossible to feel rejected by another, especially by one with whom we have felt vulnerable or with whom we have shared the deepest of experiences, and still have a positive feeling about ourselves. There is that sinking sensation that says, "I'm pretty much of a failure and not very worthwhile." If I as a person have that attitude, I'm going to project it to others and will soon begin retreating from others. Before long, I will have built a fantasy world in which I feel loved, accepted, and special. It is a defense mechanism that allows me to continue to function in a world in which I feel hurt.

If you have a problem with fantasizing, take the practical steps of working with the fantasy chart. Then take some time to investigate how you feel about yourself. Do you have a poor self-image? Are you prone to stress the negative points of your personality or looks instead of those qualities that are attractive? Is this an area in which you need to change? If so, you will find some help in our next chapter.

An Exercise in Fantasy

Deadly fantasy can be channeled into *creative* fantasy. What is the difference? The deadly kind is a make-believe world that can never become reality; the creative kind of fantasy can lead to a better tomorrow. You must expend concentrated effort and energy, however, to change from the escape fantasy world to the visionary fantasy world.

Before filling in these charts, ask God to fill your thoughts and help you turn your deadly, make-believe world of fantasy into a creative fantasy that can, with his strength, become your real world.

CHART ONE: A Beginning

When do you fantasize? Use the following chart to pinpoint your times of fantasy. Then use the Goal Chart that follows to purposely interrupt the fantasy world with concrete efforts aimed to keep you in your real world.

If you find yourself fantasizing while on the way to work in the morning, check 6-8 A.M. and note *where* you are—on a bus? train? in your car? In your goal setting, ask yourself what you could *do* with this time. Obviously you cannot read a book while driving, but you can while on train or bus.

If you fantasize during your lunch or dinner hour, you can come back to the world by using those periods to eat with someone else, and thereby get to know a new person. Remember, this exercise is mainly for those who find they want to escape from real life. *Only this "escape" fantasizing is deadly. Creative* fantasizing is fun and exciting because it can *become real.* This is what we want to aim for in the future.

Time	Place	Fantasy
6-8 A.M.		
8-12 Noon		
12-1 P.M.		
1-5 P.M.		
5-6 P.M.		
6-12 P.M.		

GOAL SETTING

Time	Place	Fantasy Replaced By
6-8 A.M.		
8-12 Noon		
12-1 P.M.		
1-5 P.M.		
6-12 P.M.		

Now, how do we move from deadly fantasy into creative fantasy? Let's look at both types a little more. We can spend our time fantasizing about male or female friends that do not actually exist; about being famous or even infamous (a lot of sexual fantasies revolve around the latter). We can fantasize about a lot of things, but if we analyze all our fantasies, we can usually see that they give us pleasure because we are *gratified* in some way through the fantasy, we are the *center of attention* in the fantasy, or we are the *one in control* of a situation or even another person.

I need to ask, then, what needs are my fantasies filling? The need to be recognized; the need to be affirmed in my person or abilities; the need to try something new or different without suffering the possible criticism of those who know me; the need to relieve the guilt I may feel about who I am, what I want, or what my life is now.

CHART TWO: Starting to Grow

Pray about every aspect of your life: your marital status, your job, your living environment, your friends, your family, the section of the country you live in. Bring your "outlets" into your prayers. For instance, do you like to travel? Do you play tennis? Are you an outdoors person or the indoor type who likes to read or putter with houseplants or other hobbies? Pray about what gives you a feeling of satisfaction. After you have spent some time praying about these matters, transfer these kinds of activities and interests to paper.

Maybe it is time for a different job, a different section of the country to live in; perhaps your interest in travel can *relate* to some dreams you dream in your *new* fantasy world. Pick up a book about a part of the country you would like to visit. Then check out some Christian organization or missionary who might live there and begin calculating how much money you need to visit that area. This is a way to begin creative fantasizing.

If a particular job is of interest to you, you might need to go back to school. Nothing will fill up your time better than taking courses. But a drudgery? Not if you see your creative fantasy becoming a reality.

Christians have one up on most of the world when it comes to *creative* fantasizing—ours can be heaven-directed! Many life-changing institutions have come into existence because of the burden of one Christian's vision that seemed like a silly fantasy to others. Isn't that the *creative* kind of fantasy *you* want in your life?

JESUS WAS A SINGLE ADULT

	Where I am Now	Where I'd like to be in			The first step I need to take
		6 months	1 year	5 years	
Marital status					
Job					
Living Environment					
Friends					
Family					
Relationship with God					
Geographical location					
Interests					
Hobbies					
Sources of satisfaction					
Sources of discomfort, irritation					

FOUR
SELF-IMAGE
(June)

A YOUNG WOMAN WITH TWO SMALL CHILDREN clutching at her slacks opened the door when I rang the bell. It had been three months since her husband had left. He had taken the family car, some of the furniture, and most of the money to begin his new life with his new woman, a woman from the same town.

Everyone knew the plight of my friend, and she had come to resent their sympathy and condolences. I couldn't help but notice how much she had changed from week to week. Her weight had increased considerably; her hair was not always combed; her house was no longer tidy.

"Come on in," she said with a faint smile. "I know the place is a mess. I just haven't had time to clean it up today."

Sharon doesn't think much of herself anymore, and it

45

shows in the way she acts, dresses, and keeps her home. The reasons for Sharon's self-image problem are evident—she has been outwardly rejected, and everyone knows it. How can she hold her head up and think well of herself?

Many singles have a self-image problem because they constantly receive an unspoken message from the world-at-large that they are second-class citizens. Frequently, singles are disproportionately taxed, have trouble establishing credit, and are viewed with suspicion by personnel managers who sometimes assume *single* means "irresponsible" and "transient."

The person alone frequently finds himself/herself excluded from group functions at work or church. Couples tend to invite couples over for an evening; often singles are hesitant to attend social gatherings, especially "dress" affairs, without an escort. After all, who wants to be the odd one in a group? In the church, the emphasis on couples' retreats, family weekends, and children's programs makes the Christian single feel uncomfortable, and the incessant matchmaking of friends doesn't help much either.

Some singles suffer because they don't have anyone close to affirm them, no one to give them any recognition on a regular basis. Others, who have allowed themselves to become so identified with a spouse or a job, crumble when death, divorce, or change intrude upon them.

THERE IS HOPE

We do not have to be overwhelmed by these feelings. One of the most encouraging aspects of practical Christianity is that we can tackle a problem, such as having a poor self-image, and can find reason for hope and a sense of direction.

But someone will be thinking that even the Scripture says we are really worthless. After all, we are told, "There is no one who is righteous," and "No one does what is right," and

"Everyone has sinned and is far away from God's saving presence" (Rom. 3:10, 12, 23).

The apostle Paul revealed this dilemma in his own life when he wrote, "I do not understand what I do; for I don't do what I would like to do, but instead what I hate. Since what I do is what I don't want to do, this shows that I agree that the Law is right. So I'm not really the one who does this thing; rather it is the sin that lives in me. . . . Even though the desire to do good is in me, I am not able to do it. I don't do the good I want to do; instead I do the evil that I do not want to do" (Rom. 7:15-19).

Reminders of the sins in our lives can cause us to give up and say, "What's the use? I can't ever measure up." One friend told us after her divorce, "My family doesn't forgive me, I can't forgive myself, so how can I expect God to have any use for me? I've let everyone down—including him."

When we feel like this, we have at least two choices: we can continue to hold this martyr's (and unbiblical) position, making life miserable for ourselves and everyone else. Or we can discover what the Bible really says about how God feels about us and what he wants us to do. Then we can explore who we are and what we can be to God, to those around us, and to ourselves.

How does God view us, and how does he feel about us after we have sinned? In Genesis 1:26 we overhear God talking: "And now we will make human beings; they will be like us and resemble us." Then we are told, "So God created human beings, making them to be like himself." When I read these statements, I realize I cannot be all that bad; after all, I am made in God's image; he has given me many qualities I can develop.

Psalm 8 sheds further light on what God thinks of us:

When I look at the sky, which you have made,
    at the moon and the stars, which you set in their places—

> what is man, that you think of him;
>   mere man, that you care for him?
> Yet you made him inferior only to yourself;
>   you crowned him with glory and honor.
> You appointed him ruler over everything you made;
>   you placed him over all creation.
>
> *Psalm 8:3-6*

What does this passage tell you? It says that as a person you have worth and value. It does not say that your worth comes from your own efforts or from your identification with a particular group or institution. Long before any government was concerned with equal rights, God declared he did not discriminate among persons on the basis of age, sex, height, weight, marital status, race, or job status. These verses say you are *not* a worm crawling on your belly on the ground; you are *not* insignificant. You were made a little lower than the angels, and you were made with the capacity to know God, to love God, and to receive his love.

"But," you say, "I have made a real mess of my life. I've gone beyond what even God could forgive." Have you done anything so much worse than shirking your work, committing adultery, and then engineering a murder? David was a man chosen by God, and he sinned greatly. But we see in Psalm 51 that he confessed his wrongdoing before God and was forgiven. He was confident that he was still of worth to himself, to others, and particularly to God.

In many of the Psalms, we see this confidence; he knew God valued and protected him.

> How I love you, Lord!
>   You are my defender.
> The Lord is my protector;
>   he is my strong fortress.
> My God is my protection,
>   and I with him am safe.

He protects me like a shield;
   he defends me and keeps me safe.
I call to the Lord,
   and he saves me from my enemies,
Praise the Lord! . . .

The danger of death was around me,
   and the grave set its trap for me.
In my trouble I called to the Lord;
   I called to my God for help.
In his temple he heard my voice;
   he listened to my cry for help. . . .

The Lord reached down from above and took hold of me;
   he pulled me out of the deep waters.
He rescued me from my powerful enemies,
   and from all those who hate me—
   they were too strong for me.
When I was in trouble, they attacked me,
   but the Lord protected me.
He helped me out of danger;
   he saved me because he was pleased with me.

Psalm 18:1-3, 5-6, 16-19

Here we have a warm picture of God's love and protection for his own. Although it is true that every unconfessed failure and sin will drive a wedge of separation between us and God, it is also true that God keeps on forgiving. God is *pleased* with us, not for our achievements, but out of his love. When we recognize this, we can move on in our relationship with him as well as look at ourselves in a more positive light.

But of course, we have to examine ourselves to be sure we are not abusing our privilege. A young Christian, who was at the time in a leadership role, told a small group of us how much he enjoyed seeing X-rated movies. He went on to explain how guilty he always felt after giving in and going to see a blue film. Then he added, "But God always forgives me."

JESUS WAS A SINGLE ADULT

That particular conversation troubles me to this day because although it stresses God's forgiveness when we confess shortcomings, it also takes glibly his admonition to watch our walk before him and to be "holy as I am holy." We want to keep in mind that on the one hand Christ continues to forgive sin, even besetting sins that haunt us time and again, and on the other hand, he will enable us to *overcome* our sins and our failures. He will, if we allow him to, give us the strength to say no to temptation. It is only when we can say, "Yes, I made a mess of _____ in my life, but I've had that out with the Lord, and now, with his strength, I'm starting in a new direction," that we can transform a poor self-image.

JESUS' MODEL

Jesus is one to whom we may look: he knew who he was and accepted his role. Sometimes I like to sit and think about him and wonder if his humanness and divinity pulled at each other. If he were wholly man (as we are told he was) and wholly God, there must have been some inner conflicts from time to time. Were there times when he wished he could take some time off to relax with Mary and Martha and Lazarus? Were there times when he wished, humanly, that the crowds would disperse and stop demanding so much of his energy and strength? We could conclude from the Gospel accounts that if he did have these wishes, he did not allow them to distort his perception of his goals.

I like his stand when he protected the holiness of the Temple by overthrowing the tables of the money changers. No pussyfooting around as to whether or not his actions would be misinterpreted. He was the Son of God, and because he knew who he was, he acted to protect and uphold the worship place of his Father. Part of his secret for maintaining a positive self-image was to stay in a close relationship to God and to see himself as God saw him.

Toward the end of his life he determined to go to Jerusalem, where he would be nailed to the cross. It was the moment for which he was born; how did he *really* face it?

"My Father, if it is possible, take this cup of suffering from me," we are told he prayed (Matt. 26: 39). We are shown his very human feelings: "Grief and anguish come over him . . . 'The sorrow in my heart is so great that it almost crushed me,' " he told his friends (Matt. 26: 38). He asked them to stay with him and support him with their own prayers while he prayed.

But instead of watching with him, they fell asleep.

He woke them once . . . twice . . . but they were tired and did not understand his grief in this hour. Finally he reached the point where he could say, "My Father, if this cup of suffering cannot be taken away unless I drink it, your will be done" (Matt. 26: 42).

At this crucial moment in his life, Jesus did not have the support or encouragement of those who lived with him. But in spite of their lack of affirmation, he was able to do what he had to. Because he knew who he was, he could make decisions, even unpopular ones, whether those closest to him understood those decisions or not. He could give love and receive love without demanding complete agreement, understanding, or performance meeting a certain standard because he had a positive self-image.

As we learn to follow his example, we will see that we are developing confidence in ourselves and a sense of our own worth and value so that we can begin to understand our own identity—separate from others, good in ourselves.

When I accept myself as a child of God, redeemed and freed by Jesus' death on the cross, I begin to see how God has established my identity. If I know Jesus Christ, then I must believe what his Word says: God made me in his image; he gave me an identity; he gave me some inherent qualities I can develop. He invites me to continue my relationship with him

51

and tells me that no matter what happens to me or to my life, I can count on there always being the opportunity to begin again if I slip. It may take some work on my part to change this intellectual knowledge into day-by-day trust; I may have to remind myself and ask others to remind me that if he is always ready to accept me, then I must be ready to accept and love myself.

REPAIR JOB

How do you go about repairing your self-image? The first thing on my list is to read daily in the Old Testament book of Deuteronomy. This book is the account of Moses' last discourses to the people of Israel before they crossed the Jordan and entered into the Promised Land. The task ahead of them was frightening, overwhelming, and so Moses reminded the people of God's majesty and intervention in their history. He recalled God's protection, direction, and love for those who belong to him.

The person with a poor self-image tends to look at the future with little hope, thinking, *I must resign myself to this situation,* or *I must make the best of it,* or *I must accept my duty even though I don't want to.*

Listen! If this is where you are, continue to read to the end of this chapter and then put this book down. Pick up a modern translation of the Old Testament and turn to Deuteronomy. Read a minimum of five chapters, and as you do, note how God gave Moses step-by-step directions for traveling through the wilderness. Your wilderness is far different from that of Moses. His was a literal wandering, yours is an emotional or perhaps a spiritual one. But as you read Moses' account of Israel's pilgrimage, complete with the people's grumbling and God's constant leading, your heart will take courage. You will be reminded of how much God has invested in you as a person and to what lengths he will stay with you in order to bring you to your own promised land.

As you read further in the Book of Deuteronomy, you will read,

> He found them wandering through a desert,
>   a desolate, wind-swept wilderness.
> He protected them and cared for them,
>   as he would protect himself.
> Like an eagle teaching its young to fly,
>   catching them safely on its spreading wings,
>   the Lord kept Israel from falling.
> The Lord alone led his people.
>
> *Deuteronomy 32:10-12*

You are the one God will lead to a new beginning. *You* are the one God will keep as he would himself (or, as another translation puts it, "as the apple of his eye"). No matter what your condition right now, no matter what your hurt, no matter how dreadful your desert place seems to be, *you* can enter—from that place—into the most challenging chapter of your entire life.

"But I am stripped of all worth, of all confidence, of all energy," you may say.

That is all right. Notice in Deuteronomy that no matter how tired the people got, no matter how often they rebelled, God never forsook them. It is only when we recognize his power and love that he will pick us up in his arms and heal our wounds and give an entirely new meaning to our lives.

The second step in improving your self-image is to look at your life as it exists. Please note that I said to look at your life *as it exists,* not as you *wish* it would exist. In other words, if you husband has died, you may wish he were still at your side, but the fact is, he is not. The same is true for the man who is alone because his wife has left him to pursue a career that will take all of her time. To want a normal life is understandable, but if that is not what currently exists, you must face that truth. For the person who has never married and is now either alone or caring for elderly parents, the probable continuation of that situation in the immediate future needs to be recognized and faced. We *must* start where we are, and we *must* realize that it is at this point Christ will meet us.

Executives often are taught about the Maslow hierarchy that suggests people have different levels of motivation. The pyramid below describes the Maslow theory and may help you see your current emotional needs:

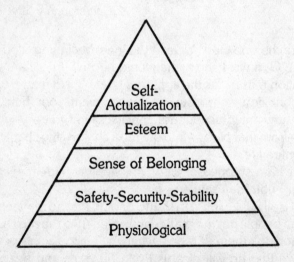

Self-Actualization

Esteem

Sense of Belonging

Safety-Security-Stability

Physiological

According to Maslow, one is motivated first from physiological needs. In other words, air, water, and basic physical needs *must* be met before a person will begin worrying about his sense of belonging or esteem. But once this physical need is met, it no longer serves to motivate an individual. That person, according to Maslow, moves to the next level. When the theory is applied to a person's career, the safety-security-stability stage means "What pension plans or retirement benefits will I have?" Once those needs have been met, the person's sense of belonging takes on more importance. In our jobs we must express our need to belong by joining the company bowling team, going out to eat with coworkers, or socializing in other ways.

Again, once this need is met, a person needs another motivation. Returning to our example of the business setting, an employee who is advancing up the corporate ladder is often given esteem through a private office, a personal secretary, and perhaps a rug for the office floor. Titles are another way of adding to an employee's esteem.

The highest motivation a person can attain, according to Maslow, is self-actualization. One need not be an executive to be self-fulfilled or self-actualized. A janitor who takes pride in making an office sparkle is just as fulfilled as the company president. An organization can create the *climate* of self-actualization and the opportunity for it, but it is only *in the person alone* that self-fulfillment and actualization can really occur.

What is the point of this description of Maslow's theory? It is included here to point out that everyone else, just like you, needs security, needs the basic elements of life (food, water, air, a roof over your head), needs recognition or esteem, needs social contacts, and needs a sense of belonging. You need to see that these needs are normal elements of every person's life.

I would modify Maslow's theory by suggesting that self-actualization comes fully into being only when Christ is allowed to take control of one's life. Believing you are important to God and that he takes personal interest in you and your life enables you to see that you have worth and can give you hope. You need to be reminded of this when you are hurting, and that is the purpose of getting into Scripture in order to see again how he has led others in the past and to what lengths he will go to give protection, direction, and guidance.

You can use the Maslow pyramid to take another look at

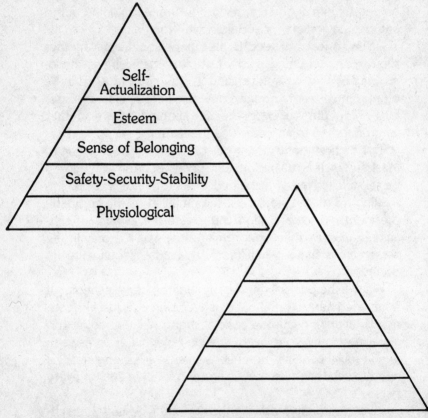

your own life. Jot down some people and places that come to mind as you look at it. Who provides for your physiological needs? Do you have a job that enables you to provide for the basic elements of your life? Is this part of your frustration—either that you *have* to work or that you cannot?

In what or in whom do you find your safety and security?

Some of us find security in having a husband or wife; for others, security is in possessions—a house, car, money in the bank. Others find their security only in God. These people usually are the most stable because physical belongings and people change, but Christ and his love and care remain constant.

Where do you have a sense of belonging? In your church? a group of friends? a commune? your office workers?

Who adds to your esteem by giving you recognition from time to time? The people whose names you have listed beside any of these areas are people who are important factors in your life. They are people you need. They are individuals to whom you can give as well as those from whom you can receive.

"But there are blanks," you say as you look at the pyramid. "One of my problems is that there is no one who really does add to my esteem!" When Sharon's husband left, she began to let herself go. Her security, her esteem, was in large part anchored in him. Now identity *should* be a part of marriage, but our ultimate sense of security and recognition must be in our relationship with God himself. He is the only factor that never changes.

As you look at the way you have filled in the pyramid diagram, you can discover at what levels your needs are being met and in what areas you still have needs. Think of the people and activities or groups whose names appear on your chart. Are there ways in which you can deepen or broaden your relationships? Think for a few moments about those levels for which you have blank spaces. What steps can you take to help that growth process?

Having looked at your life as it exists, a good next step is to think through your capabilities. My friend has a poor self-image, and yet she is a very capable mother who manages a household and cares for a family that is without a father. The fact that she keeps the budget, makes all purchases, and provides meaningful activities for her youngsters demonstrates her wide range of capabilities.

It is often helpful to take advantage of the career counseling opportunities in high schools, colleges, and adult or continuing education programs. Often women who are unhappy in their jobs or who have to return to work after years of being out of the work force find it difficult to know what field to enter. Career counseling can help a person define his or her capabilities and can help channel those talents.

Another way to improve your self-image is to treat yourself as a person who *does* have worth. When my uncle died, his wife was left alone. They had no children of their own, and she lived almost an hour's drive from our home, so although we saw her occasionally and talked with her daily on the telephone, she was by herself most of the time.

She began eating at random. Instead of setting a place for herself at the table, she would just put the frying pan down and eat from it. "All of a sudden I realized what I was doing," she told my mother and me. "I wasn't treating myself with any kind of respect at all." She went on to say that from that moment on she always made herself a good nutritious meal, set out her nice china on a tablecloth or pretty placemat, and, during the summer, even added flowers to the table. She felt better about herself because she made an effort for her own enjoyment.

To sum all this up, let us recognize that most people tend to underrate themselves and their importance to God, to those around them, and to themselves. They also tend to underrate their capabilities. God sees us from a completely different viewpoint; he sees us as individuals he loved enough to die for. Does this not mean he sees us as individuals whom he loves enough to live *in?* You are of great worth to him and to many of the people around you. Start today to take some positive steps toward expressing your worth and enjoying yourself!

FIVE
LIVING WITH YOURSELF
AND OTHERS
(Bob and June)

IN OUR FAMILY we have been on a series of visits to our dentist. I have just returned from his office where he was doing some work on a gold crown he installed in my mouth last week. He knows our efforts to write this book, and when I entered his office, he asked how it was going. I told him I was planning to write a chapter on friendship as soon as I got out of his chair and back to my typewriter.

He said, "You know, I really don't like your using the term *friendship* when you are talking about *relationships*. They are two different things."

You are well aware of how you have a discussion with a dentist who has a drill in his hand and six bales of cotton in your mouth, aren't you? He does the talking, and you grunt agreement. But we do want to talk about friendships . . . and yes, relationships.

JESUS WAS A SINGLE ADULT

CHANGING RELATIONSHIPS
(Bob)

If you are a formerly married, you can appreciate the friendship phenomenon that takes place when a mate leaves his/her partner either by death or divorce. One day, it may be six months or two years later, you realize that all your former friends are no longer there. You take an inventory and begin to wonder, "Where did all the people go?"

I am amazed whenever I watch the crowds at a sports event. It takes a crowd of 50,000 people several hours to gather for a professional football game. They arrive in campers sometimes six hours before starting time, all ready to spend the day. But in less than fifteen minutes after the game is over, the stadium is empty and everyone is running toward the nearest interstate highway. If you are a formerly married, the gun went off when he or she departed from your side. Now you probably have observed that the interstate highways around you are filled with former friends all seeking their way home, while you sit in the stadium of emotions alone, wondering why the game had to end so soon.

The single person watches as friends marry, and soon those frequent get-togethers are fewer and fewer. After a period of time, your relationship is down to receiving a Christmas card. You ask yourself, "Am I the one who has changed so much that my friends have left me?" The widow or divorcee who had many friends for the years of marriage now finds the social life of all those friends no longer includes her. Has she really changed so much that they do not want her?

Recently June and I did an all-day seminar on the subject of "Beginning Again." As a result of our preparation for this workshop, we became very much aware that many of the friends we have had in our singles' group are no longer close to us. I began to ask myself the question, "Why is it that people we love and have spent hours with have seemed to fade into the past without a word?"

After a great deal of introspection, we came to the conclusion that it is not that they do not want our friendship, but that they no longer need it. In most cases this is very healthy. I can think of one woman with whom we must have spent between fifty and sixty hours in counseling. We have not heard from her in six months.

What is the difference? Her life is changing, not ours. Recently we learned that she is to remarry. Her whole future is now exciting, and the bitter days of divorce and anger are gone. She has made new friends based on the relationship she has with her fiance and her family. Not long ago, June called her; she was just bubbling about her life and future. She was not angry with us; she was very much in love with us as a couple, but her life and her needs were different.

We have had to learn that we cannot cling to the relationships we once had with individuals in our group. When they come to the Christian Singles Foundation, they are going through the process of heartache and bitterness. They look to our group as an oasis in their desert of grief and bitterness. Once that period has passed, and they are on their way to complete healing, their tendency is to move away from us into their own new lives. That is how it ought to be . . . but sometimes when they go, we are hurt.

What does all this mean to the single who sits at home and waits for the phone to ring or for the doorbell to chime? The key word throughout this chapter is *change*. You are changing, along with your friends. Or, perhaps it is not you as much as it is your relationships.

If you are in the process of a divorce, your relationship to others is changing every day. Can you remember when you got married and many of your single friends no longer had priority in your life? Now you are embarking into a new relationship with many of your former friends. Remember that not long ago you were part of a couple. You acted, thought, and behaved like a part of a couple. Today you are *not* part of a couple; you are a new unit, a formerly married single, and many in your former circle of friends don't know how to handle you. For instance, when you were part of a couple, it was understood that you would not violate the law of the jungle and steal someone else's mate. Now the jungle is not sure how you will act.

We've centered on divorced people in our comments so far, but the person who has lost a mate by death has the same experience. You suddenly find yourself a threat to some of the marriages around you, and to some measure this is also true for the never-married single. You may discover that Jim and Alice are not quite the lovely couple they pretended to be when you were once part of a couple. Jim or John or Harry will visit you, without his Alice or Mary or Jane on his arm. He feels very sorry for you and offers any assistance you may need; however, his view of need is not the leaky faucet in the kitchen but rather your sexual and physical needs.

For the men reading this material, don't be too surprised if insecure Alice one day shows up at your doorstep with a casserole. Be careful that the casserole does not have the hook called, "Can I help you relieve any physical tension you may be suffering?" At this point, you need to realize that friendship has gone down the drain, and you are facing exploitation. An offer like this may turn you on for the moment, but if you are like most of the people we have counseled, you will wake up one day sick with yourself, your actions, and your so-called friend.

Can you think of friendships that are changing for you? It may be in your own family or with your in-laws. You may see changes in your church relationships. Changes occur in community and civic groups. Perhaps in your business world you have also noticed changes in your friendships and relationships.

What is a friend? If you can find a friend who is willing to share those last difficult hours with you before your "betrayal," you have found a dear friend. A friend is one who makes no demands in return for his friendship. A friend can share, not just in words, but in being with you and supporting you with his/her love and presence. Jesus did not long for a discussion or lecture from any of the disciples when he withdrew to pray in Gethsemane. He wanted their support and presence for his hour of trial. He withdrew to have his privacy with the Father. As a man, Jesus was lonely and wanted someone to share his final hours of pain.

I hasten to add that privacy is very different from loneliness. When I was widowed, there were times when I wanted my privacy and there were times when I wanted someone to share my loneliness.

What does one do to maintain a normal life under the conditions of changing relationships and changing friends? Our advice is to not compromise the person you are and were. You must first become a friend to yourself all over again. Do you like yourself the way you are now? If not, you need to start there. If you are a never-married single and gave up on yourself years ago, that's where you need to start. If you have just come through a divorce, you are probably still licking your hurts and really don't like yourself too much. If you are widowed, your fear and guilt over things you wish you had done better in your marriage are telling you that maybe you are not all that worthwhile.

Once you have taken a good look at yourself, think of a friend who will make no demands, give no sermons, but will listen well. (A word of caution here: men should think of *men* friends at this point and women, *women* friends!) Go to that friend and say, "I need to unload about five years of grief, anger, and garbage on you. Can you take it?"

If he or she will, begin to talk. Hopefully this friend will become someone who, if it is necessary later on, can look you straight in the eye and say, "What are you doing, dating that creep?" This friend is one to whom you can tell the truth, who will listen in confidence, and when asked, will give you an honest opinion. We all need a friend like that.

Our greatest friend of all is Jesus Christ. If it were not for the spiritual strength I received from him, I do not believe I would have made it through my struggles after my first wife died. We are spiritual people as well as human beings. The one thing Jesus never gave up in his hour of trial was prayer. He could give up his friends who fell asleep during his struggle, but he never gave up his one link with the Father—his prayer life.

You may say, "I don't have a spiritual base or prayer life to build on." If this is the case, seek out someone who can begin to introduce you to a personal walk with the person of Jesus Christ.

I like to believe that Psalm 23 is the singles' psalm. You can substitute any word you want for the word "valley" in that Psalm, and you can see how God is promising to walk with you. Jesus is not a once-a-week counselor or psychologist. He says he wants to be Lord. I take that to mean a 24-hour-a-day leadership role in my life. Only when we understand that we must submit to him, the one who loves us because he is love, do we find his strength and companionship to lead us through the valley of divorce, death, or loneliness.

LOVE IS HARD WORK
(June)

The last time I sat in the dentist's chair, my mouth open wide as he drilled, I listened to our philosopher-friend talk about the need to know yourself and the need to be realistic about the way you live. He got started on this topic because he knows Bob and I have a lot of friends who are divorced and because his brother had just called to say he was leaving his wife.

"He's bored," the dentist said, referring to his brother. "He thinks if he can say 'I love you' to someone new, things will be different. What he doesn't realize is that we bring our hang-ups, our guilts, our problems from one situation into another. We all need to come to grips with reality. I think we need to know who we are, what we realistically can expect from life, and we need to stop living in our fantasy worlds."

My dentist friend is right. I might debate with him about where a realistic view ends and where Christ and the supernatural enter, but in a good, common-sense fashion, this man sees the picture.

Love, as it is described in books, magazines, television programs, movies, and theatre productions, is fantasy. It is constantly exciting, continually sexy, and bears little recognition to what we know to be true. It is a brittle love that comes apart easily. For all the commercial glamor that says love can outlive anything, we usually refuse to give love that chance. The moment it stops giving pleasure or demands more than we feel like giving, we want out.

Our pastor's wife is a very wise woman. One time when she and her husband addressed a group of singles on the subject of love and marriage, she told us how much she loved her husband. She then went on to say, however, that if she had never met him, but in the course of time met someone else she respected and loved to a lesser degree, she could have made a good marriage with that individual. Her point: Love is *hard work*. It is a commitment. It means staying with the job of building a life together in the good times and in the not so good times. It isn't a matter of giving fifty percent or sixty percent or seventy-five percent effort, it means giving one hundred percent *all the time*.

We all need to learn how to love like that. The single who is alone and has no children to care for can find someone who needs and wants this kind of love. The single with someone—a child, parents, or others—can learn to give that

65

JESUS WAS A SINGLE ADULT

one hundred percent kind of love even if he has been hurt.

"But I *did* that," someone may be saying, "and all I got was a slap in the face."

The slaps do come. Undeserved, ill-timed, when we least expect them. But can we let them stop us from giving the kind of love Christ exhibited and calls on us to give? Christians are called not only to love one another inside the church but also to speak to the world by loving it with all its callousness.

But *what is love?* The song of a few years ago said, "Love is just a four-letter word." We have said it is, among other things, commitment. Where is love? How do I find it? To whom may I give the love I have within me?

Love is usually thought to involve only the relationship between two members of the opposite sex, or between parents and children or family members. But isn't love really more than this? Isn't it the love, in a wholesome sense, that I have for my own self and worth combined with my affirming another person and then interacting on a deep level?

We have a friend who is an excellent model for this kind of love. She is a hospital nurse who stands out to patients and staff alike because of her genuine care for each patient with whom she has contact. She listens, she looks into the eyes of the individuals she nurses, she speaks to them with concern and kindness.

I worked at Park Street Church in Boston for a number of years. As part of the staff of that very large city church I was privileged to meet a wide variety of people. A special time in our church life centered around the ten-day missionary conference the last week of April each year. At one of these conferences, a missionary who had been on the Park Street roster of supported individuals was scheduled to be at the church for the first time in many, many years. On the first day of the conference, the chairwoman of the week's events paced nervously back and forth in front of my office. It seemed no one had seen this missionary for fifteen or twenty years, and no one could quite picture what she looked like or knew much about her as a person. I, too, began to anxiously await this woman's arrival—more out of curiosity than real interest.

The picture I conjured up in my mind as I waited for my first look at this lady was of a prim little woman who resembled the scrawny, white-haired, tight-lipped typing teacher I had in high school!

All day long as the missionaries and the guest speakers from around the world arrived with their luggage, I listened for the name of each female entering the door. Finally the door opened and in walked a chunky gray-haired woman in her late forties. She had a quick smile and a ready "hello" as she asked directions to the conference chairwoman's office. It was the missionary we had all waited to meet and she proved to be worth waiting for.

In one of her first messages during the conference, this lady told us how she became a Christian and later a missionary. She had come from a well-to-do family and, if I recall correctly, had been engaged. When things didn't work out, she got into her car and drove as fast as she could, deliberately planning to veer off the road at a certain bend in the highway so that she would catapult down into a huge cavern. "Without warning, the car came to a screeching halt," she told her captured audience. "It just died, and I found myself slowing down and rolling to a stop. At that moment I was overcome with the realization that God must love me very much to prevent me from taking my life and that there must be something I was spared to do."

This woman became a missionary, working with delinquent boys. She had us roaring hilariously as she recounted stories of literally tackling one young lad as he tried to escape from the home. Other times she had us in tears as she shared moving stories of broken and renewed relationships. During those ten days our missionary taught us that it is possible to transfer the need to receive love and the need to give love from a sexual context to a whole different plane of life. She had found an outlet to express herself, and in return, many young people who found their lives turned around because of her influence had given her their love.

Does this mean we are all destined to be missionaries if we are single? Not any more than if we are married. I sometimes resent the inference that all single women have been "saved" by God to go to the foreign mission field. Many of them have found the Lord leading them in that direction, but that is not the course for all. I do believe, however, that God places people in our lives whom we can love and by whom we will be loved in return.

The bottleneck for most of us seeking an avenue of love is our determination to find that person or persons who will love us back. This drive prevents most of us from letting out the love we have. It is only when we can give it without thought of what we will receive in return that we really learn what love is. Only at the point of giving will we learn what love flowing back to us can be.

Each of us has limitations. A person who is financially handicapped learns to live within certain financial means. It takes time, it takes hard work to make ends meet, but a person can learn to so live as to be happy. The hard-of-hearing individual learns to read lips and can function with a minimum of difficulty in a world of sound. The emotionally uptight man or woman must learn how to pace himself/herself in order to achieve stability. No matter who we are, no matter what our life situation, we can learn to enjoy life, have fun, find meaningful relationships, and know what *love* means.

One single woman we know adopted two small children. This lady had never married but was able to take in these two little girls and make them hers. It was not easy. After some years she had to give them up, but her desire to give her love away was important, and she channeled it into the life of two youngsters for as long as she was able.

A man whose first wife died, whose son died, and whose second wife divorced him, is alone. But he, too, has found young people to whom he gives himself as he seeks to help those afflicted with the same disease that took the life of his son.

A young woman in a university setting unobtrusively moves into the life of student after student, often young married couples, and helps them with their living situations. She has a gift of listening as they describe their adjustment problems, and she enhances young life after young life. She gives, and people love her in return.

I once attended a conference at which the leader had us study 1 Thessalonians 1 from the Phillips translation. He centered on Paul's admonition, "Love is hard work," and periodically during the 2½-day seminar would bellow out, "What is love?" and thirty of us would send back a resounding chorus of "Hard work!"

The lesson stuck. True love doesn't resemble the limp, shallow characterization of the word we often give it; love is hard work. But love is deep and rewarding for those who seek it and share it.

DEFEATING LONELINESS
(June)

The need for love heightens our sense of loneliness. Loneliness is like a hammer pounding us deeper into ourselves, splintering the very core of our self-confidence. Feeling lonely is very different from being alone. Solitude can be enjoyable—there is time to think, to rest, to do something special. Being alone can be enjoyable; being *lonely* never is.

Before I was married, I used to think that loneliness didn't exist for couples. I learned this was not true. Loneliness faces everyone, married or not. For the formerly married the feeling is intensified because of the close, intimate union the individual has experienced. When those intimate times have been taken away, a person suffers intense emotional pain.

When are the lonely times for you? A man might think of coming home to a dark, empty house at the end of a day's work. For a woman it may be the hour after the children leave for school in the morning. For the never-married person it may be Saturday night or Sunday afternoon. Some of the lonely times are predictable, others surge to the surface in unexpected moments—a song on the radio, an old photograph tucked away in a drawer, a spring afternoon when it would be fun to go for a walk with someone special.

To be lonely and yet not find a way to deal with the loneliness that sometimes engulfs us is to allow this emotion to govern our lives.

A middle-aged woman said to Bob one day, "I get so lonely it propels me to pick up a guy, any *kind* of a guy, just to feel the warmth of a man next to me." She went on to say of how little worth she felt herself once the short liaison was over. This woman recognized the intensity of the loneliness she felt but could not handle it constructively.

Many of us have the same problem. Our outlet may not run to the severe limit our friend's did, but we still allow our feelings to control our actions. Some make constant trips to the refrigerator, or glue themselves to a television set. Others sink more and more often into a world of fantasy where people exist who care. Still others retreat into sleep.

Before I was married, I found the loneliest time of the week was Sunday afternoon. Saturday nights didn't bother me very much, but Sunday afternoons never seemed to end. I was involved in my church, which had full morning and evening Sunday programs. After dinner I often would lie down to take a nap—not so much because I was tired (although my weeks were very busy)—but because it was a way to pass hours that dragged. My naps were an escape from a lonely block of time I didn't want to face.

Loneliness can force us to go window-shopping. Being where the merchandise is, we often purchase a treat for ourselves, justifying our action by saying it was necessary in order to pick up our sagging spirits.

All the above *are* outlets for loneliness; but are they constructive outlets? I don't mean to infer that it is always wrong to take a nap, or to go shopping, or to watch a television program, or to enjoy a hot fudge sundae when we feel down; but if we *always* react this way, then our loneliness is in control. For our own emotional well-being, we need to turn the situation around so we learn to control our loneliness rather than to be subject to its tyranny.

Let's go back to the question of what are the lonely times for you? Is there a way to offset them? Your own imagination will help you in this area, but let me suggest a few ideas to get your thinking started.

One man we know eased the loneliness of coming home to a dark house by setting an automatic timer. Ten or fifteen minutes before he pulled into the driveway, a lamp switched on and a radio began playing. Just opening the door to the sound of music and a light in his living room gave him a whole different perspective for the evening. True, no one was there to share his sight and sound, but the initial loneliness barrier that confronted him every night was gone.

A woman I know turns on the television or radio—not so much to actually listen to a program as to hear other voices. "I can't stand being indoors any other way," she has said. Here is a person who recognizes the emotion she feels and counteracts it by taking a positive step. I might add that because she listens to talk shows and news, she is well versed in many subjects and therefore finds it quite easy to make conversation when she is with other people.

Instead of taking to the living room couch every Sunday

afternoon, I would have been far better off to start jogging or ride my bicycle. Nothing works off frustration, loneliness, and anxiety quicker than good physical exercise! The lonelier I feel, or the more unhappy I am with my existence, the more tired I find myself. The more tired I feel, the more inclined I am not to want to go out, and so the cycle goes on.

Similarly, one-night stands or short-term physical relationships are no answer to the problem; ultimately, they cause more, not less, anxiety, guilt, and loneliness. We defeat ourselves by succumbing to our feelings rather than finding a way to work them out in a healthy manner.

Giving to others is one of the best ways to conquer loneliness. Work on giving love. There are Big Sister and Big Brother organizations that demand a commitment of so many hours per week for those who indicate a desire to befriend a young girl or boy. There are deaf people who can communicate with only one or two other individuals, because few people have taken the opportunity to learn how to sign. There are political campaigns and charities that need volunteers.

If you insist that this type of involvement is *not* your bag, go to school. Learn something just for fun, or enroll in a career counseling group in a local college if you wish to pursue a new career. Career counseling can give you insights to more than your job opportunities. Often you can take tests that show you strengths and weaknesses in your personality, give you helpful hints on how to improve your strengths, or give you ideas about your capabilities that you did not know were possibilities.

A friend of ours said recently that one of the most helpful suggestions she could give to others who have experienced the death of a marriage would be to try something new. One of the psychological needs that every human being possesses is the need for new experiences. To do something different, to try something you haven't dared try before—whether it be traveling to a foreign country for a month or taking tennis lessons—will help overcome besetting loneliness.

What new experience would you like to give yourself? Set a realistic timetable for achieving it, and then move from the loneliness you feel toward that goal.

Here are some steps you may wish to follow.

1. Determine the times you feel particularly lonely.

2. Decide what new experience you are going to undertake. Don't neglect the question of enough physical exercise. (I *don't* get enough exercise and, as a result, have started attending the Early Bird Swim at 7:00 A.M. at the local Y and have found it a great way to start the day. Sound crazy? Maybe. But if you try adding something *really new* to your routine, you will find it an overwhelming stimulus.)

3. If your lonely times include the early hours of the morning when there is no pool or tennis court open, use this time to read literature relative to your new venture.

4. Sign up for lessons, or solicit a friend's involvement in your new undertaking.

5. *Begin!* And be mature enough to give your new adventure a chance. If you enroll in a course and after three weeks decide you don't like it, finish it anyway. And even if you *do* enjoy it, start thinking *now* about the next experience you will pursue once the current one has become a part of your past history.

SIX

HARD THOUGHTS ON A TENDER SUBJECT... SEX

(Bob)

CAN YOU THINK OF A SUBJECT that causes more raised eyebrows, more curiosity, more debate than sex?

For centuries, fulfillment in life was equated with marriage and family, and being single meant remaining sexually alone. Remarks such as "You can never miss what you've never had" were snide, ignorant innuendos meant to put the single down. Today, things are different.

The world at large assumes singles are not sexually pure. Live-in relationships, one-night stands, and the occasional short-term arrangement are common alternatives to the more straight, traditional life-style. After all, isn't sex normal? Shouldn't everyone want to be part of an intimate relationship? Whom does it hurt? It no longer seems to matter if singles, even as young as high-school students, satisfy their sexual desires. Birth control methods have taken away the fear of pregnancy, and with the fear has gone any sense of wrongdoing for both the man and the woman. In many cases, women have become the sexual aggressors.

It would be naive for us to assume that the halls of the church are free from these attitudes. Christian married persons and Christian singles have often been caught in the web of sexual sin. Some 50 to 60 percent of the singles coming into the church have engaged in sexual activity outside of the marriage relationship. A good number of Christian divorced persons, as well as the majority of non-Christian divorcees, have yielded to their physical desires and have been involved in sexual activity since their divorce.

BE HOLY

In previous chapters, we have talked about the need we all feel for love and about the battle we have all fought with loneliness. These, coupled with our own sexual drives and the pressure from the world to conform to its standards, provide plenty of opportunity for us to have problems with our sexual responses. These pressures increase for the formerly marrieds who have previously enjoyed a satisfying sex life.

What reasons can we give for singles not expressing and finding fulfillment for their physical desires?

First, the New Testament plainly teaches that sexual expression is to be reserved for marriage and that marriage is holy. In fact, the bonds of marriage are compared in Ephesians to the relationship Jesus Christ has with the body of believers. In that illustration we learn how close and intimate Christ wants to be with those who belong to him, and we learn the divine potential for a full marriage relationship.

When we tamper with sex outside of marriage, we are

reducing the Church to a slut or harlot, and we are making Christ "one of the boys," interested only in satisfying himself. But Jesus does not take the Church at will, he does not call her for one-night stands, and he does not love her only when she is lovely or loves him in return.

There are strict admonitions in Scripture to set ourselves apart and treat our bodies and relationships as holy. There are still some people who hold to the biblical belief that the privileges of sexual relationships are limited to marriage. Those who oppose that belief seem to have little understanding of the cost of having a sexual relationship without the support of marriage.

In a recent conversation with a group of singles, the question was raised as to whether or not it is wrong for singles to sleep with married persons (which implied it is all right for them to sleep with other singles). Most of the group felt it was wrong because the married person was not being honest with his spouse. I offered the suggestion that such preoccupation with the sex aspect in any relationship is totally false, because sex is such a minute part of the full relationship people can have with one another. My comment was based on a statement in Gordon MacDonald's book, *Magnificent Marriage*. The author states, "The lowest form of communication is physical or sexual. One may immediately disagree, recalling many intimate moments of deepening love and endearment. But the physical level of communication for people is so significant because of the other levels of relationship which are blended into the physical experience. Isolate the physical level from all others on a communications basis, and you have only the instinctive exercise of procreation."

When a man and a woman have a sexual encounter outside the marriage bond, they have established an emotional relationship without providing for its care and nurture. In our society, the act of intercourse has been heralded as the ultimate in a relationship. To deny that there is pleasure in intercourse would be an injustice to God's goodness and creative purpose. But the physical encounter, outside a structure of commitment, only exploits and then degrades those who participate.

The shortest course toward an emotional shipwreck is to get involved in a sexual relationship without the protection of marriage. The single person with an empty house or apartment who goes out seeking company risks a prostitution of his emotion that is far greater than any physical act. All too often the price for companionship and laughter is a night between the bedsheets. But when the sheets cool off and the mate for the evening has left, the old loneliness is still there—with a great fury of frustration and despair.

THE DISCIPLINE OF COMMITMENT

One underlying theme must be repeated again and again. Love is *commitment;* sex is *commitment.* Commitment is commitment *only* when it is *life-long.* Marriage is not all roses; it is based on a pledge to each other out of which love and relationship grow.

We recently read an article in a personnel journal about the lack of employee commitment. If a young professional goes skiing for the weekend and the forecast is for new snow and better skiing on Monday, the journal said such an employee will call in sick from the ski lodge. He will most readily choose to enjoy his sport rather than honor his professional obligations. By the same standard, if a woman cannot get a hairdresser's appointment until 11:00 A.M. on Friday, she will frequently call in and boldly state she will be late. This kind of philosophy also says, "I want all the privileges of marriage: companionship, sex, love, and security, without the commitment of a long-term obligation." Studies are now beginning to show that persons who have come through several of these "convenience" marriages have difficulty maintaining any long-term commitment to a person or function, whether social or professional.

A local radio station interviewed a rabbi about his views on the breakdown of marriage in America today. He said that love is a growing relationship. Growing takes time; growing needs a protective structure.

When we got married in 1973, we felt a love for one another. We thought we loved each other deeply; but as we look back, we can see how much our love has grown in the five years we have been husband and wife. In 1973, I did not know what it meant for me to make the bed and put on a pot of coffee. Five years later I know that simple acts of kindness say, "I love you" just as much as any evening of sexual sharing. Although not all expressions of love are as enjoyable as others, they are all necessary to build up a strong relationship.

The one-night stands, the convenience agreements, all say that as long as you feed me whipped cream, buy me roses, and keep the good juices flowing, I will be with you. We have known couples who have been married fifty and sixty years. They don't go around kissing each other on the back of the neck, like the college kids do on the Boston subway; but if you look deeper, you can see a simple look or a wink that speaks of a whole life of love. My parents will observe their fiftieth wedding anniversary in another year. As we notice little things about their lives together, such as the fact that Dad now makes the beds and dusts the furniture, we realize that we who say we love each other after only a few years of marriage, have just started down the path of romance.

One day, I was teasing June and said, "When you reach 40, I may trade you in for two twenties!"

My minister was in on the conversation, and he quickly answered, "Be careful; you may not be wired for 220."

We know many couples who seem to have come to an emotional time in their relationship when they are looking for two twenties or 220's. What has gone wrong? Does love need to be recharged like a fading battery? We have already said that love is hard work. It is, in fact, a relationship that requires work on a day-by-day basis. Part of that work is a deep commitment to each other in which each looks out for the other's interest. There are millions of people whose only commitment to a job or position is because of the money. No marriage is going to work with that type of commitment as its foundation.

We have decided that keeping a marriage growing is like the secret of building and keeping a fire going in the living room fireplace. My brother-in-law gave us a special air convection grate, which is a little higher than the normal fireplace grate. We have learned after many hours of blowing and paper burning that we must supply the underneath section of the grill with the proper kindling in order to start the fire, and then we have to keep an adequate supply of wood burning below the grate in order to burn the larger logs on the surface. Whenever we neglect to feed the smaller fire, the larger blaze dies out. It doesn't do any good to add more wood or use the bellows on the logs. We have to go back and rework the fire at the foundation.

We thought of that grate again a few months ago. We had arrived early at a local college and began to set up the seminar room we would use for our workshop. As we worked, we chatted with the college custodian. He asked what we were going to discuss, and we told him we were speaking to the formerly married about "Beginning Again."

He replied, "I don't have to worry. The wife and I have worked on our marriage for over thirty years. We knew one day the kids would be gone, so we made a special effort to keep our love for each other current and active." There are millions of divorced persons who have paid billions of dollars to counselors and psychiatrists because they never understood that simple formula.

We can begin to see some reasons why Scripture forbids sex outside of marriage. The intimacy of the physical encounter produces an emotional relationship that can only be developed in an atmosphere of commitment and selflessness.

FACING REALITY

Understanding some of the reasons for meeting God's standards is only one of the helps we have at our disposal.

If we look at ourselves, we can begin to see (in a negative sense) what our misuse of sex is doing to us, and (in a positive sense) we can focus in on the realities of who we are, where we have been, and where we are going.

We know of one woman who was a very active church worker and a godly person. When her husband left her for another woman, she lost total control of herself and became a street harlot. She was sleeping with anyone who would open a door. One day, as she tells it, she realized what she was doing. She was taking her anger out on herself, and she was destroying herself. She was angry with God. She was angry with her husband. She was angry at the church, because she felt it had forsaken her. The method she used to retaliate was to exploit herself as a sex object. Today, this woman is very thankful that the God with whom she was so angry did not turn his back on her.

The emotional state one finds himself in when he has been betrayed by the one who loved him can be destructive. If, in retaliation, that person exploits sex as a way out of his misery, he can be ground down to total defeat.

A young woman came to our home one night to tell us that after her husband had left her, she was emotionally devastated. He went to live with his lover, and the wife filed for divorce. Coming from a Roman Catholic background, she knew she was going against the teaching of her church. Out of emotional hurt and a feeling of self-pity, she, too, started sleeping around with different men. She was trying to convince herself that she was still attractive and desirable.

She stood in our living room, looking out the picture window and said, "First my husband rejected me for another woman, then the church rejected me because I was divorced. I went to confession one night but could not face the priest for fear he would reject me. Then when I started sleeping around, I found that once the act of sex was over, those men didn't want me either. Finally I rejected myself. Now I am at the point of suicide."

The first reality we face in our humanness is that when we seek to find acceptance by the use of sex, we will only find exploitation and, ultimately, rejection. Now that we have faced such a reality, we are still left with the frustrations and the fact that we *do* have sex drives! To deny this fact is to deceive ourselves.

Unfortunately, too many Christians feel guilty about admitting they experience normal sex desires. They fear they will be looked upon as evil or out of control. Every question related to the sex urge seems inappropriate to discuss.

Take, for example, the act of masturbation. It is possible that a large majority of married persons have masturbated without their marriage partner involved. But let the single person even *discuss* the subject, and immediately he is labeled strange, sexually perverted, or homosexual. We are neither condemning nor condoning masturbation; we are merely making the point that people often will not discuss any aspect of sex that could have personal implications.

If there is one area in which the Christian single bears the greatest attack by Satan, it is in this one. The work of Satan is always to defile what God has intended to be pure and constructive in the life of his children. Sex is not sin. Temptation is not sin. But yielding to the sexual temptations that come into your mind *is* sin.

JESUS WAS A SINGLE ADULT

It is most important to recognize that Satan is at work to pervert your sex life. Some may think that we are saying that sex is evil. Not at all! Sex is good, beautiful, and exciting. In its proper place, it is the ultimate conclusion to a meaningful relationship between a husband and wife. Outside the bonds of marriage, however, it is contrary to the will of God.

When we were at a singles meeting in Boston and made a similar statement, a woman in her mid-thirties proceeded to quiz us, because she felt such a statement was unrealistic. She was formerly married, had enjoyed an active sex life when she was married, and felt that she should not now deny herself in this area of life. My experience of being a widower made me especially sensitive to her comments. I agreed with her that from a human standpoint the desire and need does not change. However, God's standard for sexual purity is one we must uphold. "If I change," I said, "or society changes, that does not mean that God's standard for purity changes." I then asked her what her standards were for the way her sixteen-year-old daughter handled her sexual drives. The fact that we have physical drives does not give us license to claim that they are always a "God-given" appetite that should always be fulfilled.

BUT WHAT DO I DO?

It would be foolish to list a series of guidelines for persons on what to do and what not to do. If you need some, go to any Christian bookstore, and pick up a book on sex advice for teenagers. Apply the suggestions to your life at this point, recognizing that in this very emotional area, we are all rather adolescent.

But how do we handle our sex drives and needs in the light of the standard of purity set forth in God's Word?

Recently a Christian psychologist spoke to the members of our Christian Singles Foundation and recommended we learn the positive benefits of sublimation.

If you want to sit home and read *Playboy* or *Playgirl,* then you are setting yourself up for mental intercourse, having a sex life that is not yours. On the other hand, if you decide to use your time and strength working toward a constructive goal that will use up your energy and leave you tired when you arrive home at night, you will be on a safer road. There are many worthwhile projects and activities in which we all could invest ourselves.

One meaningful and very healthy way to cope with physical desire is to start running—both physically and mentally. Joseph ran when Potiphar's wife made advances to him. Joseph's running was to flee temptation; we need to remember that *there is a time to run.* By expending physical energy, Joseph was helping to deal with his own temptation as well as avoiding the source of that temptation. Remember, temptation comes most often when we are bored, tired, or depressed. When those feelings come, we need to put on the tennis shoes and literally join Joseph's jogging club.

There's an old adage that says if you do not want to smell like a barn, you must not live in one. We cannot deal with sexual temptation by encouraging it. If we swallow the line that by going to see a lot of X-rated movies, we are fulfilling our sexual needs, we are deceiving ourselves. The only way to get steam up in a furance is to ignite the fire under the cool water. If we watch a movie in which a man and woman are in bed with each other engaged in sexual activity, we light the match to our sensory boilers. This is really the point of Joseph's fleeing from Potiphar's wife.

On the other hand, we can count on the fact that Satan is not going to bombard our sexual desires at a prayer meeting. He could put some sexual thoughts in our minds if we saw an attractive person of the opposite sex, but be sure he attacks only on his terms and usually in his own territory, where he is free to destroy.

Let me add a word of caution here: Christians ought not to delude themselves into thinking that a man and woman can get away to a quiet place together for the purpose of sharing "spiritual truths" and not be faced with sexual temptations. You may smile at such a warning, but people have done so with good intentions and found themselves *without* their jogging shoes!

One helpful method to fight mental temptation is to recognize that while I am not abnormal to have sexual thoughts, I need to be sure those thoughts do not remain in my mind. I have found the best broom for an impure thought life is to memorize Scripture.

When I find I am going off the deep end in mental sex sins, I quote verses to myself. Some will say this is denial. It may well be, but it is the best way I know to clean up a mind that is being tempted in this most vulnerable area.

I have found that working in a university setting as I presently do, even though there is a great deal of sexual activity between students, there seems to be a trend in favor of self-respect and less meaningless sex binges.

Where else can one find total self-respect than in a full and meaningful relationship with the God who loves us and has made us in his own image? Jesus Christ came to give us back our self-respect in the areas of temptation and weakness. By following God's standard and God's Word, we not only bring peace of mind to our hearts, but we can feel good about ourselves.

In my own experience of widowhood I was faced with the temptation of sexual sin. But then I thought, *I was faithful to myself and to God in my youth and in my marriage. Why would it be so impossible to be faithful to God now that my wife is dead?* It was difficult, but not impossible. I found that God in his strength is the same yesterday, today, and forever.

The point to remember is that we must be close to him, not the world. If we as Christians hover around the world's fringe activities to "watch" or to "be more aware of life," the pull will eventually carry us from the fringes to the center of activity. Our wholeness comes when we choose to follow Jesus rather than the world.

SEVEN

SPECIAL PROBLEMS OF THE FORMERLY MARRIED
(Bob)

SOME TIME AGO, NBC ran a television movie called *Breaking Up.* It was about a woman who went on a picnic one afternoon with her husband and two children, only to learn between sandwiches that hubby was unhappy and wanted a separation.

The program was a good portrayal of what a woman and her family go through during a separation and, ultimately, a divorce. Most viewers who had gone through similar situations would probably say the grand style in which the man was able to support his family was unrealistic, but other parts of the story would ring true.

As the movie pointed out, the major problems for the

formerly married are loneliness, sex, hustlers and plastic people, financial and legal difficulties, and family responsibilities. Of course, all the problems of life and the world are summed up in those words. But when the ingredient of being formerly married is added, the problem is multiplied tenfold.

ALONE . . . AND AVAILABLE?

The stereotype of the formerly married woman being fair game for every unhappy male is not too far from the truth. A single friend told us of her experience during a recent political campaign. One of the local selectmen knocked on her door to solicit her vote in the upcoming election; but before his visit was over, his campaign had turned from votes to personal favors, with an invitation for cocktails, campaign work at night, and several other fringe benefits a married selectman could offer a very attractive divorcee.

This type of situation has been written about with enough frequency in the past few years that we do not have to waste much ink on it here, except to say that five years ago we would have been warning women about the Mr. Machos lurking in the bushes. Today, however, both sexes are potential victims of sexual hustlers. The female on the move can be just as bold as any male.

Being warned is forearmed; we don't *have* to be an object used to fulfill someone else's pleasure. If an encounter or a relationship has started to head in what you know to be a wrong direction, it's never too late to put on the brakes and give a firm, unconditional, "No thanks." Of course, we need to be sure our words, actions, and attitudes aren't sending out "come-on" signals. Sometimes it is to ourselves that we need to say *No* first of all!

One of the most difficult adjustments for me in my widowhood was to go to bed with only a cold pillow next to me after experiencing love and affection for many years. Some formerly marrieds we have known try to solve the empty-bed problem with a one-night lover or by establishing a new, although not permanent, relationship. But when the night or the relationship ends, they have come away full of guilt and with an even deeper coldness in their hearts.

The bed is not the only place where one is alone. The kitchen table, once the center of chitchat and fun, becomes an echo chamber of lonely hours broken only by FM music.

Within the past few years, programs have been developed to help individuals face death and dying and loneliness. Although most of these workshops come out of a secular context and occasionally suggest options not available to Christians, they can be of real help to the Christian facing the crisis situation that sometimes develops out of acute loneliness.

We have mentioned in other chapters some of the positive steps the single Christian can take to begin overcoming the problems of being alone. Here we would only add our encouragement to develop within your own church or fellowship group the kind of loneliness workshop or clinic we have mentioned and add it to the unique perspective of the Christian hope.

FACING FINANCIAL REALITY

Although we will deal with finances in a later chapter, we need to mention a few things about our attitudes and expectations in regard to money matters. In the movie *Breaking Up,* the protagonist packs her bags and leaves for New York. Her father makes a few telephone calls, and she lands a starter job that eventually leads to her big breakthrough. She reaches the point at which she can tell her former husband, "I like me. Now I want to stay the way I am." I cannot fault the idea, but movies do tend to exaggerate reality. Most women we have met have been forced to take, and to keep, rather routine types of employment.

One woman called to tell us she was going to receive a certain amount of alimony from her husband, along with half of their savings. All she had to do was manage to keep her head above water until the divorce was final, and she would be in fairly good financial condition.

"What if your husband doesn't pay his alimony?" I asked.

"He has to, or he'll go to jail."

My answer was not what she wanted to hear: "If you send him to jail, he has no job. Secondly, the courts are so busy they cannot even keep murderers in jail for long . . . do you expect the bureaucratic system in this confused world to worry about whether or not you are receiving your support?"

This sounds cruel, but unfortunately, it is very true. We urged her to start seeking employment that could lead to a professional career. We told her to take some definite, positive steps *that day* and *not* to wait for the pot of gold at the end of the divorce settlement.

Often a widowed or divorced woman will encounter discrimination when she looks for work. Not only does she have to fight for equal pay for equal work, but she also has to deal with the new subtlety of having money come in from other sources such as alimony or, in the case of the widow, insurance. Although it is illegal for a company to justify a lower salary because of secondary income, some women have found themselves so penalized but have felt they must tolerate the injustice in order to keep a job.

When you enter the job market, you need to be aware of the normal salary ranges for the kind of positions you are interested in. Your public librarian can help you locate these statistics for your locality; newspaper advertisements will also provide some information. Most jobs do have a fixed salary range; the exact point on that scale, however, is negotiable. Remember, questions of salary and your future financial expectations with a company need to be discussed and understood *before* you take a job.

YOUR ATTORNEY

Many people feel that a lawyer is an expert in all fields and that any lawyer can handle all problems. Much like the medical profession, however, lawyers today are becoming more and more specialized. For example, if you want to draw up an estate plan, you would not go to an attorney who is a noted criminal lawyer. Most firms today have three or four lawyers in their office, each with diverse backgrounds.

If you are like the average person, you have dealt with a lawyer at specific times in your life. Perhaps you have had a will drawn by a lawyer or had a lawyer present when you bought your first home. But very few of us have had a lot of contact with an attorney, and our lack of knowledge has led to the Perry Mason image of lawyers—honest, works hard, and handles only one case at a time with his staff of seven assistants.

The average person filing for separation or divorce often does not realize that his/her lawyer may have as many as fifty or seventy-five cases waiting for a hearing in court. As our British friends say, it is necessary to "cue" up and wait in line for your day, not only in court but in the attention of the person whose desk is piled high with the papers of those seventy-four other cases.

Unfortunately, Perry Mason never told the public what his fees were for the type of service he supposedly rendered. I am amazed at the disparity in legal charges. Some attorneys advertise in the local newspapers "Divorce—Uncontested—$200." On the other hand, I was told by a young woman going through the divorce process that she was paying $2,500 for her divorce because she had the best attorney in the city. I don't know how good this attorney was, but I surely know that her fees are the best in the area!

In today's market, the average attorney will charge around $50 per hour. The bigger firms will charge $75. Most attorneys will require some form of deposit, ranging from one-third to one-half of the total fee to handle a divorce. Some will state a flat fee, while others will quote an hourly figure. Many people who come to us are hurt to realize that when they have called their lawyer for minor advice, that call has been charged to their bill. We have pointed out that lawyers are like taxis—their meters run whenever you use their services!

Most persons who are thinking of divorce or separation are usually hurting from the combat of a poor marriage. They do not want to struggle with a lawyer who is supposed to be resolving their other woes. But in too many cases, the legal process becomes another battleground. A woman called us one evening to complain about her lawyer. "He won't return my calls, and I just can't get any action on getting a settlement for myself and the children," she sobbed.

In another instance, a woman's lawyer agreed with her husband's lawyer to give him a cash advance from the couple's joint savings account at the time of the settlement, the amount was to be repaid.

When the divorce was finalized and the agreements were signed, all parties involved forgot the $500. A few days later the woman remembered the initial agreement and called her attorney. His answer was, "Well, no one is perfect. Forget it."

At this point our counsel to the woman was to pay the lawyer's fee, minus the $500, and to put a P.S. on the bill that read, "No one is perfect . . ."!

How do you choose an attorney? Use the same method as if you were new to a community and wanted to select a dentist, doctor, barber, or shoemaker. First, get recommendations from people who have used an attorney. Don't depend on just one or two recommendations; a quality lawyer will have a consistent reputation. *Do not use relatives or friends.* This can only create another set of strained emotions. You are free to investigate a person who is a professional. If you do not know a soul, go to the local police department and other authorities and ask about the reputation of Lawyer X. If you know absolutely nothing about a lawyer, call your local or state legal aid for assistance.

Once you have decided, go visit the lawyer. Do not judge a book by its cover. I have one attorney who still uses his grandfather's furniture, but I would trust him with my life. I also know of some very borderline attorneys who spend more money on interior decoration than on legal books.

Discuss very frankly the fees and how you will have to pay them. If you have a financial problem, be open with your attorney. Find out if the calls you make to him will be included in your bill. If you are required to put down a deposit, determine if it is part of the total fee. *By all means, have your agreement put into writing.* Of all people, a lawyer knows that verbal agreements are hard to prove in any court. You would like to assume you will not have any problems with your own attorney, but remember, if you are going through a divorce, you are going through some very difficult and emotional days. Protect yourself by having all the facts put in writing so there will be no question later.

Once you retain your attorney, let him or her handle your case. Stay out of the legal battles and do not try to deal with your spouse or spouse's attorney. This does not mean that you do not work with your attorney to get what you feel is proper for you and your family. The law is a very strange animal at times. I have been amazed that the court does not always rule in favor of things that seem very logical to a layman. What you say, even if you have your emotions under control, may be used to your disadvantage. Add this illogical pattern to the emotional upheaval of divorce, and you can readily see why it is necessary to have a good lawyer you can trust.

Many people ask us, "Do you know a good Christian lawyer who will handle my divorce?" How do we answer that one? It is hard enough to find a good Christian lawyer who will draw up a will, to say nothing of taking a divorce case. Most of the Christian attorneys we know don't handle divorces—it is not their area of speciality. But there must be some who do.

One warning, however, should be issued. As in any profession, just because a person is a Christian does not mean he or she will represent you to your satisfaction. I am sure that my style of professional work offends some Christians I deal with. Our humanness is usually greatly exposed on the day-to-day basis of sweating out our living. Knowing someone is a Christian or has a reputation for being a good church member is not necessarily the same as knowing he or she is the attorney who would best represent you. You still need to do your homework!

CHILDREN

Probably the most difficult part of being a formerly married single is to try to be both parents to your children if they are with you; or to maintain a relationship that is not strained, if they are with your former spouse.

After a long struggle, a friend of ours left his home once his wife decided their marriage was over. He moved out, leaving the children behind with their mother. One afternoon we asked him how it was going. His eyes became cloudy as he said, "It's not the same." He went on to say that he had taken his daughter to the shopping center the night before, and it was then that he noticed how strained his relationship with the little girl had become and how difficult it was for them to relate. He was no longer a part of the child's everyday world, and he found them drifting apart. "I don't know how to change it," he said.

As this friend talked, another man came to mind. His wife had died, and he was left with the responsibility of rearing their four children, one of whom was now a teenager. "I travel a lot," he had told us, "and when I'm home, all the teenager and I do is fight. I don't like the kind of kids he is relating to, I don't like the way he talks, and I don't like the way he dresses."

Our friend was angry at the boy and resentful that he was left alone with the enormous responsibility of rearing his children. He was in a complete quandary as to how to change what was happening under his own roof.

"I hate coming home," he added dejectedly. "The boy is influencing the younger children, and I don't know where to turn. It consumes all my strength just to try to deal with this one problem."

Another friend of ours is a middle-aged mother with teen-age girls. "They cut school and all Joni wants to do is to get a car. I'm against it at this age, but her father has promised to buy her one. What can I do to stop him? He won't listen. He wants to make sure the kids still like him, and so he buys them what they want. It completely destroys all I try to teach them every day."

A younger woman with smaller children recounted the story of her husband's suicide. As she finished her story, she looked up and said, "You know, my childhood was filled with love and laughter. Not long ago I was looking at my four children, and suddenly I realized how different the atmosphere is for them from what it was in my home. I grew up with four sisters, and we laughed a lot as a family. My children never laugh. It makes me ache."

Can you think back to your childhood and remember a disturbing event other than the death or divorce of a parent? I can still remember the day when, as a very young child, my mother took me shopping. We traveled by bus to the shopping center and, as a treat, she bought me a bag of balloons. This was a special gift to me, and my little heart was excited. But when it came time to get off the bus, I was so busy making sure I was close by my mother's side that I left the bag of balloons on the seat. I can still remember the heartache within me as I stood in the street and watched the bus pull away with my precious treasure. For days I would return to that same street corner, watching for the bus and hoping that the driver would recognize me and give me back my bag of balloons.

What a small example of hurt and loss! Can we really know how the loss of a loved one affects the heart of a child? How can we adequately explain death or divorce to a child? From our family experience, I can say that several years after their mother's death, our children still do not find it easy to discuss her death or the events surrounding it.

We remember the old axiom, "Don't judge another man's journey until you have walked in his moccasins." In the case of children, it is impossible for us as adults to even put the moccasins on our feet, no less walk in them. The emotions, conceptions, and fears are there every day in bold reality.

Can you imagine some of the questions that run through a little mind when the child finds out that mommy or daddy has died? *Was I a bad girl? Why did God punish me and take away mommy? If I am good, will she come back? Was mommy unhappy with me? Did daddy really love me?*

Often teenagers are even more affected by the loss of a parent, especially in a divorce situation. For all the outward casualness exhibited by some young people, the inner hurt can be seen in their eyes, in their attitudes, insecurities, and lack of self-confidence. And all of these feelings manifest themselves in behavior.

Dr. J. Allan Petersen, in *The Marriage Affair,* states that one of the greatest needs of children is to see that the parents love each other. When June and I were married several years ago, we approached our marriage and our new relationship with the children with the thought that June was my wife first, and not a substitute mother. It was very difficult for her to adjust to *four* people instead of just one (me!) at the beginning of our marriage. But only as we were rightly related could we give the children what they needed. Children's basic need is security. This simple word is very complex in its application. Can children find security in a home torn by divorce? We believe it is possible to heal the wounds of many years of combat or feelings of desertion or guilt, but it is not easy.

Giving children security enables them to relax in their own world. When a father or mother has disappeared from their lives, much of their security is in knowing that the remaining partner cares enough to discipline them. The lack of discipline in a home says to the child, "I really don't care how you live your life, and I won't take the time to help you grow up into a mature adult."

Security is also knowing that not *everything* is going to change. One little boy cried when his father left and finally blurted out, *"I can't* be the man of the family." He felt a world of pressure pushing down on him—not a pressure from his mother, but the pressure of his own mind as he looked at his younger brothers and sisters and knew they no longer had someone "in charge" at home. He was frightened by the demands he *thought* might be placed on him and frightened that he could not meet those demands.

Part of security for any one of us is stability or constancy. The person going through a divorce may say, "How can things be stable in the midst of this kind of situation?" Of course the main structure of the family is being changed when one of the parents is suddenly missing, but there are other things that can be continued to give a measure of stability.

Don't neglect the things that have been meaningful in the past. Visit grandparents, go to the zoo or beach, or do whatever has been the norm for your family. Don't let the ghosts of the past prohibit you from sharing in the wonderful memories your children have. I am amazed how, some six years after my first wife's death, the children still reflect on some happy experience we had as a family eight or ten years ago.

We need to emphasize that one of the greatest stabilizing factors in your child's life is *you*. You must take special care of yourself in all phases of life. If you begin to neglect yourself physically, mentally, or spiritually, it will ultimately affect your child's life as well as your own.

If two widowed or divorced persons, both of whom have children, marry, they need to remember these security needs. In all of the efforts to mesh your two families together, you must take care to preserve the treasures of the past as well as work toward the point where one group of children can begin to be taught to start sharing those treasures with their new brothers and sisters. For instance, camping may have been extremely important to one family, and the intrusion of the new family members into what is "mine" may be a threat at first. To wait a year or two before jumping into a two-week camping vacation for the new, enlarged family might be wise.

After the need for security comes the need for sensitivity. We take our burdens to our friends, our minister, or a professional. Our children have very little opportunity to open up and share with anyone about their feelings (unless the child is under professional care). In many cases, the parent is too busy with his or her own adjustment problems to see the need of the children in this way.

When one friend of ours was able to mention to her teenage son that seeing a counselor was helping her deal with her divorce, he quickly said, "I wish *I* had someone to talk to." She heard that plea and immediately asked if he would like to try talking to a counselor. His answer was yes, and it opened up a new understanding and area of communication between them. Some may not be able to afford a professional counselor, but perhaps there is a person in your church or office who would be able to befriend your youngster. You will need to remind yourself often that confidences between that adult and your child *must* be kept.

In contrast to the sensitivity area, there is also the need for a parent to convey strength—not the steel, rigid, domineering attitude that some might think of, but rather a positive, moral standard of life that is conveyed to the children. The Scriptures instruct us to train up a child in the way he should go. In my mind, this is the parent investing his or her life in leading a child in a proper way of life.

Have you ever entered a major highway and been at a loss to know the speed limit? Do you know the feeling of looking into your rearview mirror only to find a State police car following you? Many of our children are growing up on a life-style highway with no maps for their journey.

The father of a man I know raised his children in an atmosphere of Christian love and guidance. When his son went into the military, he took on a new life-style and broke his father's heart. Finally his father wrote and said a very difficult thing to his son. He told him he could not accept the young man's life-style but that he still loved him. He also told him that if he was going to continue living a life that was contrary to God's standards, he wished the son would change his name.

Later the son related how it broke his heart to receive such a message from the father he loved so dearly. It was a shock wave that made him stop and evaluate his life and where he was going. Today, that young man is a dynamic Christian leader who was turned around at that point in his life because he saw the value his father placed on certain standards.

Can such a statement backfire? Yes. But we have confidence that we can pray for the Spirit's haunting persistence in a young life that will eventually bring him or her back. For some it has taken years of such prayer, but the Lord has proved faithful.

BEGINNING AGAIN

For many, beginning a new life as a formerly married single requires a five-year program that includes both short and long-term goals. The immediate short-term goal is *survival,* a means of seeing your way through the day-by-day bills and pressures. As soon as possible you need to begin an upgrading program on your way toward a longer-range goal. You might need to go back to school or get professional refreshing in the case of a nurse, teacher, artist, or any specialist.

If you can allow yourself the luxury of a five-year program, it will help you deal with the tendency to hope that tomorrow you will meet Mr. or Ms. Right. We have known both men and women who have never given up on the hope that they will remarry very quickly. They have put off making plans for their future and are living in a "holding pattern."

Unfortunately, we have found that for every nice single out in the wilderness there are ten con artists waiting to take advantage of you. We don't want to frighten you; but you do need to be cautious, even in the church. Humanity is often exposed as we are finding our way back after a divorce or death of a spouse, and the matching/mating games that often take place within the church halls can be to the detriment of the formerly married.

If for no other reason, this breather period will give you the opportunity to discover yourself and gain self-confidence. By giving yourself some time to grow, you will have more to offer a future mate and will have a better perspective from which to view your possibilities.

GO SLOW

The person who has just come through a death or divorce situation must be careful not to jump into another marriage too quickly. You need time to get to know the person you have become since your widowhood or divorce and to determine the direction of your life. If you find, after a period of time, that you have met someone you want to share your life with, don't move hastily, but follow a few rules that might help to insure the longevity of your future relationship:

1. Get away with some friends for a weekend, or travel with some other people. See how your prospective future mate interacts with you and your friends. Seeing him/her in this kind of context will help you to know that person better, especially if he/she acts differently than you expected.

2. Discuss the issue of your intimate needs, desires, likes, and dislikes before marriage. If you don't, you could be in for a very negative experience.

3. Don't sell all your property the first week of your new marriage. If you own a home or other property, wait for six months or a year before you merge your assets. For a small fee, you can have a will drawn up to cover a one-year period of your new marriage. We have known several couples who have remarried, sold all their individual possessions, and pooled their funds only to find the problem of allocating these joint funds caused havoc in their new relationship.

"But we are *Christians*," you may answer. Yes, we know. But unfortunately, we who name the name of Christ don't always *live* the way we should. As difficult as these words are to write, and as difficult as it may be for you to read them, we urge you to be careful in this area.

EVALUATE

Finally, we cannot say too often how important the input from other objective, but caring, people can be.

Both June and I deal with personnel situations in our professional lives, and we are used to the performance review process. Many employees fear a performance review;

for them it is like going to the dentist—he may have to hurt you in order to help you. But when employees look at reviews as a process to expose their strengths and weaknesses so that a program of corrective action can be designed to help them do a better job and grow as a person, they realize the value of such a process.

Unfortunately, many of us are fearful employees in the area of seeking constructive criticism and advice when it comes to our lives, marriage, children, financial, or sexual matters. But to seek advice and be willing to consider these highly personal matters in an open way for our *own* review is both healthy and helpful.

There are many sources of counselors: those in private practice and those connected with counseling centers in colleges, hospitals, and churches are some obvious people to seek out. But many times you will not need a professional. If you know an individual with integrity in your church or small group, who has the gift of listening, and is able to ask questions that will help you explore your alternatives, you probably have all you need. In fact, you can even take yourself through a review performance session—all you'll need is paper, pencil, and some time alone.

Whichever way you go, remember that it is only as we identify problem areas that we are able to change them.

EIGHT
MONEY GAMES
(Bob)

WITHIN THE PAST FEW YEARS, most states have developed some form of lottery system. In Massachusetts one of these is called The Game. Thousands of individuals buy tickets and hope to win a million dollars in this gigantic money game.

I often think of the many singles we have met who are caught up in the *real* money game—trying to survive from day to day.

We live in a spending (or charging) society. One of the subtle traps we have fallen into in our nation is the desire to keep up with the family next door. To do this, husbands and wives both work. But what happens if death or divorce destroys that financial partnership?

A typical case would be the experience of Mary and John.

John is a schoolteacher making about $18,000 a year with his summer work and coaching responsibilities. Mary was fortunate enough to finish her education, earning her R.N. before she and John were married. Now that the children have come along, Mary tries to work three days a week to bring in an extra five or six thousand a year. They are just getting by, looking forward to the day when the car payments will stop and the orthodontic work is finished.

One day John comes home and announces he is leaving; he wants a divorce. Eighteen months later, the divorce is final, and Mary is on her own with the kids. Soon she realizes she must work full time in order to support her children, because what John is sending her is not even enough to provide all the required food for the family. It becomes apparent to Mary that she cannot afford to keep the house and must sell it (if indeed she has been able to hold onto it during the divorce proceedings).

She sits down, calculates her year's expenses, and determines that the equity in the house will hold her over for a year or so and will help buy the new car she needs for work.

Mary begins to look for an apartment only to find that they cost as much or even more than her house payments. Most of the apartments she can afford are too small to be comfortable for her family or are in neighborhoods she would rather not live in.

She has to weigh the cost of a comfortable neighborhood against her need to work full time and, therefore, to leave the children alone for long periods of time after school. Does she trust her children in this location with their neighbors?

She finally sells her home and moves into an apartment, only to find her lawyer gently reminding her that she now has to pay a capital gains tax on the sale of her house.

Mary pays off the bank, the gains tax, the legal fees incurred, and sees she has just about enough to repair the old car and hope it will run another 50,000 miles.

If we were to make Mary the villain in our story and put John in the supporting role, we would find he is just as poorly off financially.

Some of you can identify with this illustration. In most divorce cases, the living standard of the person caring for the children drops two and sometimes three levels. The divorce rate is highest in the middle class, those people who were taught to hate welfare and have too much pride to apply for it. Or, if they have applied for it, they feel ashamed and sometimes guilty.

In the case of a partner's death, the financial crisis comes on more slowly. Usually there is some life insurance to help for the first few months, while in a divorce situation those months are the worst financially.

When I became a widower, I became very impulsive and would want to spend just for the sake of doing something. At one point, I had an overwhelming urge to buy a Corvette. I had justified how I could afford it and had convinced myself that with three kids I could always use the second car for family needs. Fortunately, I never did yield to that drive, but it was an insistent force in my life for many months.

A friend of ours who was widowed at 25 after only a few months of marriage shared the same type of experience. With this woman, however, her "corvette" syndrome was clothing. When she felt depressed, it was time for a new dress.

We have talked with both men and women who have made all sorts of impulsive financial decisions immediately after the death of their mates. This symptom is easy to understand in the light of the normal lack of emotional resistance.

The never-married single is sometimes stereotyped as having all the pocket cash necessary to have a good time. A few jet-setters may fit this picture, but the average single person has to plan and to budget.

In addition to the more obvious problems of making a

paycheck stretch far enough, the never-married person faces certain other money-related pressures. Some become trapped in jobs they don't particularly like because they want the fringe benefits the company offers: retirement funds, pensions, health insurance, dental plans. "I have to take care of myself," a young man said. "I've moved around considerably, but now it is time to think of the future." This attitude may become even more important to a woman. "Things are fine now, but the question of who will take care of me at the end of the line is something that is always lurking at the back of my mind," one friend said. "I have to plan now how I will be cared for if I become infirm when I am old."

While this attitude holds true for some, others let their jobs sap all their time and energy. In their search to find something to which they can give themselves completely, they become workaholics. These individuals have so identified themselves with their work that they have, for all intents and purposes, lost their own identity.

Many singles find themselves living in a holding pattern instead of getting on with life while they are waiting for the right person to come along. A single woman often puts off buying her china or silver until she is engaged. Men, too, often put off major investments until they decide to settle down.

One friend of ours upset her family when she told them of her plans to buy a house. "They cannot understand why I would want to do something like that before I marry. What they cannot seem to see is that I'm over thirty, may never marry, and I've come to accept that. I want a house of my own, my own furniture, and things I enjoy around me; but the whole concept confuses and upsets them." She is a person who has determined not to live in the future, holding off certain things she would like to do until there is a ring on her left hand. But many singles feel that to take this step ties them down and would not give them the freedom to move quickly if a potential marriage mate comes into their lives.

The harsh reality of the financial crunch can be severe enough to put some individuals under deep depression. If you have ever been down to your last dollar, while the bills and expenses kept coming in, you understand this point well. Some can say, "Let the bills ride." But how long does that attitude last when the second and third overdue notice comes?

The value system we have been taught over a twenty- or thirty-year period through our parents, church, and general upbringing usually prevents the average person from tossing the whole matter off without a care.

Is there an easy answer to some of these problems? I believe every case has to be taken individually, and no one answer can be applied to everyone. What we have found, however, that is most needed at times of financial stress is to have a second or third party listen to your situation and to advise whether or not you are taking the right steps.

In my professional work as a financial development officer for nonprofit organizations, I have been fortunate to receive some training in finances and estate planning. One need not be a lawyer or banker to advise someone not to spend more money than he or she has in the bank or in equity.

Find someone with personal integrity who either has professional training in the financial field or who has demonstrated sound common sense in the practical issues of life. Be willing to share the details of your assets and debts and to take seriously the advice of this objective observer.

When you are faced with any crisis that demands a monetary outlay, seek the help of a competent friend. Don't fall for the quick advice of a stranger. Last year we met a woman who needed the chimney on her home repaired. She didn't check the references of the individual she contracted to do the work. She gave him the $500 deposit he requested on the work, which he estimated would cost $1,000. He worked for her one day, cashed the check, stole several dozen concrete blocks from her yard, and never returned.

Some may think, "I would never be taken in like that." We would remind you that in the pressure to get a job done or a problem taken care of, it is easy to be taken advantage of by self-seeking individuals.

The first solution that comes to mind for many widows and divorcees is to rent out a room in order to increase their income. We have witnessed, however, some sad situations that have developed from this action. One person we knew found that the young woman renting one of her rooms had a steady male caller who was at the house while the owner was at work. This incident caused our friend grief and constant concern until finally the young roomer left . . . with her boyfriend.

It is so important to be careful about anyone you bring into your home after the death of a mate or a marriage. At the time my wife died, my business commitments caused me to be away from home many evenings. I was concerned about leaving the children alone, and so I began to spread the word that I needed a person to help with the meals and care for the youngsters until I came home. Among the offers that came included those from women who said they would not only cook and babysit but for a few extra dollars would also satisfy my sexual needs.

I am grateful to the Lord that he protected me during this type of temptation. During the period right after my wife's death I was emotionally and physically uptight. It would have been so easy to arrange for such convenient companionship, but fortunately the Lord protected me in my weakness.

Go back with me for a moment to the woman who took in the young female roomer. At first their relationship was fine. The young woman provided companionship for our friend just when she needed it most. Our good friend was not an old woman by any means, and her divorce was emotionally crippling. It took some six months for her to regain her ability to deal with herself, no less other external problems.

The room and board situation worked well—until the boyfriend moved in during the day. Our friend who owned the house found herself in a dilemma. She needed the money the young girl paid, but spiritually and emotionally she could not handle the relationship taking place under her roof between this young woman and her male companion. What was the result? Our friend would lie in bed, boiling inside, just as she did during her divorce situation. Anger, fear, hurt, and broken trust marched through her room at two and three in the morning, mocking her and her decision-making powers. Finally she mustered the courage to tell the young woman to leave. But the experience drained her in a time when she had little emotional strain left.

Not all housing experiences are negative. We know another young woman who bought a very large home for the purpose of providing rooms for students from a nearby Christian college. The friendship and love she and her little boy received from these students helped heal many of the wounds she had suffered from her divorce.

BALANCING THE BUDGET

For the formerly married, the day-by-day operation of a family budget can develop into a deadly weight around one's neck. In some cases the person never handled the financial matters while married and is at a complete loss now that circumstances *force* him or her to assume responsibility for the monthly bills.

In my own situation, my job was to manage an organization's budget, but my wife loved managing the home budget. I was pleased with this arrangement. Wally did a fabulous job and made our budget survive every crisis. Then one day I was widowed and had to face the checkbook. I opened the first month's bills in panic. What had been paid? When does the semiannual real estate tax bill come in? What about our insurance charges? In what period of the month do I deduct them? On and on it went. Even though I was a financial professional, I had to learn to conquer these problems.

Recently I became acquainted with a young Christian woman who rode the commuter train with me. She knew a lady I worked with, and so we developed a friendship over the many miles of railroad tracks that we journeyed each day.

One day the young woman came into the train with a smile on her face and a lovely diamond ring on her left hand. Her engagement now opened a whole new area of conversation for us. I mentioned to her one day the need for her and her fiance to create a budget and stick with it during the early years of their marriage. I drew up some simple ideas and a system for them to follow, even giving them some accounting paper on which to chart their income and monthly obligations. About two weeks later she appeared on the train very shaken. She told me that when she and her fiance had tried to work out a six-month budget, they had wound up in a big battle, upsetting them both. She was ashamed of having cried so much over silly old money when they were not even married yet!

There are no secrets in developing a budget. What one must be sure to do is to include every item you can possibly think of that will be your responsibility in the near future to pay.

At this point I must make a distinction between the single, never-married person who has been used to a certain life-style for several years, and the recently widowed or divorced person. The never-married person will be used to a certain level of spending and knows fairly well what he or she can afford to do in any one year. But, I would hasten to add, most of us need the discipline and help a budget offers.

The widowed person hopefully has some life insurance on

which to depend for the first few months of his or her single venture. Adjusting to the single life and running a home on your own is easier if you have a few thousand dollars extra to see you through that first year of financial surprises. My caution here is to use a budget to keep you from wasting a great deal of funds. When my wife died, I spent some two or three thousand dollars for which I still cannot account. I did not engage in any unusual activities that would cause such a large spending spree; I spent these monies as "emergencies" arose to keep from adding to my grief or concerns.

The divorced person will find a completely different set of circumstances. In some cases you will actually be fighting for the very dollars you thought you and your mate had saved together. In many divorces, the mates become adversaries on the battleground of finances.

I can remember the case of one woman who had agreed to a settlement for her divorce. In lieu of alimony she got the house and summer cottage. The savings accounts were split, and both parties appeared happy. As the year progressed, however, she began to receive the tax bills, the repair bills, the insurance bills, and many other items that she had never given thought to at the time of the settlement.

You say simply, "Well, sell the house or the cottage." She could not, because the divorce was not final. Her former husband would not sign any papers to release any of the property until the divorce was final. For some eighteen months this woman had to struggle and scrape up every penny she could find to survive—even with all of her assets!

I would suggest, if you are in a pressured financial situation, that you ask a local banker for professional advice. Usually a second mortgage or open note can be secured to carry you through such a period of adjustment.

Now that we have given a quick overview of some of the early pitfalls that you could stumble upon, let us begin to think about an annual budget.

SETTING UP A BUDGET

First, it is helpful to take all the checks you have written in a previous year and sort them out into stacks you can classify as annual, semiannual, quarterly, monthly, and miscellaneous. If you don't have your checks (you should keep them for three or four years to satisfy any tax audit you may have to pass through), you can use the checkbook entry ledger that hopefully you have kept in the bottom of your desk or your dresser. Take several sheets of paper and give them the same headings you would if you had the checks.

Annual expenses: List some of the items you *know* will come to you once a year and mark the approximate due date. These obligations could include home insurance, real estate taxes, auto insurance, and in some states, personal property tax on cars, boats, etc.

Certain life and health insurance is billed annually. Call your agent for details. If you get the runaround, find a new agent. The insurance business is very competitive, and someone will be very happy to service your needs. One word of caution, however, about changing home insurance and some car insurance. Some policies are three-year policies, and to change company midstream could cause you to suffer paying a premium. In the case of auto insurance, be careful of your driving record. If you have had one or two accidents, which often happens during a grief period, you may find it difficult to obtain a policy with a new company.

When working with annual expenses, there are at least two ways to build them into your budget. Let's take the real estate tax on your home. If the tax bill for your home is twelve hundred dollars a year, you can either pay this amount out of some nest egg you have put away, or you will have to budget $100 monthly and DO NOT TOUCH that money no matter what happens to you.

It is helpful for budgeting purposes for your bank to deduct this tax along with your mortgage payment, but you should check to see if you are getting paid any interest on the funds the bank is holding in your tax account. If they *do* pay you interest (which some states now require by law), find out the amount. Never feel that you are too dumb to find out such matters. This is how you build your independence and confidence in your ability to do things on your own.

Again, if you find your banker seems to put you down, go find one who will take time to explain your business dealings in a way you can understand. Remember the key is that where there is competition, someone is always willing to win your business, as small as it may be. There is no reason to stay with an agent or service person who is indifferent to your needs.

Under annual expense you may wish to list your vacation expenses and set aside money for it either monthly or quarterly. Take a vacation, no matter if it is only a trip to the next town to spend a weekend at the Howard Johnson's Motor Lodge.

Semiannual expenses: Most of the above items would serve as a good checklist for searching out semiannual expenses as well. I can only think of one other, and that is my water bill from the town. Many city or town expenses are billed semiannually. If you are not sure what the procedure is in your area, call your town or city hall to be certain. Some real estate taxes are payable twice a year, and some of our automobile insurance policies are semiannual premiums. If these payments are too severe on your budget, in most cases, you can get them changed to quarterly with only a minor fee for the service.

Monthly: Most of your accounts will be settled on a monthly basis. This is fine if you get paid once a month and so do not have the temptation to spend your money as soon as you receive it. But most people are paid twice a month or weekly and you have to fight the battle of spending on a weekly needs basis. Try to organize your bill paying and spend on a monthly concept. Let me list a sample of monthly obligations from my budget.

Monthly insurance (Life) draft
House payment
Auto payment
Church giving
Telephone
Department store charges
Electric bill
Heating bill
Auto credit cards (gas)
Travel and train expenses
Food and household needs
Recreation

In addition to these regular charges, I must budget for my quarterly and semiannual payments as mentioned before.

Real estate taxes ($_____ /month)
Auto insurance costs
Savings account
Home insurance
Family life insurance
College education costs

This is by no means a total list of expenses you will encounter; your budget expenses will differ from mine. The point of this exercise is to be sure you have included *all* your major expenses so you are not surprised with a one thousand dollar expense mid-way through your budget year.

The unbudgeted, reckless spending of $20 or $25 a week for which you have not allowed will destroy your financial plans. For example, house repairs should be included if you maintain a home. I estimate that I spend about $50 a month on minor repairs around the house. When you break that

PRELIMINARY FACT SHEET FOR ANNUAL BUDGET—19___

ANNUAL BILLS	AMT.	SEMI-ANNUAL	AMT.	QUARTERLY BILLS	AMT.	MONTHLY BILLS	AMT.	WEEKLY	AMT.	MISC.	AMT.
Family life ins	$360	Real est. taxes	$800	Auto ins.	$210	House mortg.	$205	Food	$75	Christmas	$200
Auto license	10	Water	30	Life ins.	50	Electric	22	Church	20	Vacation	300
Charities	200	Dentist	50	United Fund	10	Telephone	16	Travel	12	Birthdays	100
Lawyer's fee	100	Doctor	50	Auto repairs	40	Gas. cr. cards	30	Entertain.	15	Plumber	100
						Master Charge	20	Dry Clean.	5	Appl. Rep.	100
						Sears, Roebuck	17				
						Auto loan	87				
						Druggist	15				
						House repairs	10				
						Clothing	30				
TOTALS	$670		$930		$310		$512		$137		$800
1 for year	$670	2 for year	$1860	4 for year	$1240	12 for year	$6144	52 for year	$7124	1 for year	$800

Column 1	$670
Column 2	1,860
Column 3	1,240
Column 4	6,144
Column 5	7,124
Column 6	800
TOTAL	$17,838

Expenses	Weekly	Monthly	Quarterly	Semi-Annual	Annuals and Misc.	TOTALS
Jan.	137 x 4	512	210	50	50	
Feb.	137 x 4	512	50		50	
March	137 x 5	512	10	800	360	
April	137 x 4	512	40	30	50	
May	137 x 5	512	210		50	
June	137 x 4	512	50	50	200	
July	137 x 4	512	10	50	300	
Aug.	137 x 5	512	40		150	
Sept.	137 x 4	512	210		100	
Oct.	137 x 5	512	50	800	50	
Nov.	137 x 4	512	10	30	10	
Dec.	137 x 4	512	40	50	200	
SUB. TOTAL	7124	6144	1240	1860	1470	
EXPENSES						17838
SAVINGS		1200				1200
EDUC. FUND			2500			2500
TOTAL EXPENSE	$7124	$7344	$3740	$1860	$670	$21538

Estimated total expenses for the year $21,538
Divide by frequency of salary payments 21,538
   divided by 24 (twice a month) 897.42
Semi monthly take-home salary must be $900 to meet this budget.

In order to follow the above budget, one would need an income of some $30,000 per year before taxes. For most singles, you will have to adjust to your own income and expenses.

down, it is only $12 a week, which does not go very far these days in a paint or hardware store. Along the same line, your medical and social expenses should be considered. If you plan to take your children to one event a month, you must figure that event into your plans.

By this time you may be saying, "I cannot keep up with all this; I might as well give up." Remember the important thing is *to start*. Sure, we all forget some items. When you discover an oversight, build it into your budget immediately.

The purpose of financial planning is to control spending. Most people reading this book will not have unlimited incomes. If you do, you too will want a budget, because by controlling your resources you permit intelligent growth. With a budget, you will be able to forecast within a few dollars the amount of income you will have each month. What is vital is that you do not outspend that income in your month-to-month obligations.

If after adding up your monthly obligations, you find that you are $30-$40 overspent, you can be sure that you will be several hundred dollars in the hole by the end of the year. What do you do when you come up $40 a month short? You can't ask for a raise, because your personal situation has no merit with your employer. If you take a second job (which many try as a solution), you find that expenses for child care and food go even higher while your performance on your primary job deteriorates.

A few years ago, a local bank used an ad that said, "When you cannot afford to raise the bridge, you must lower the water." Evaluate your situation and seek ways to cut your spending. I do *not* mean to *delay* your spending—the American mind says if you can't buy something now, charge it! But the bills come in eventually, and you are in the same predicament of looking for those extra funds to meet expenses.

One of the most difficult characteristics to maintain during the stress of a divorce or the loss of a loved one by death is self-discipline. A budget is the day-by-day test of self-discipline. It is the last thing in the world you want to worry about on a daily basis. I do know that it is the one item that, if neglected, will cause some of your greatest pain over a prolonged period of time.

If you are looking for a budget guide, you can find one in most well-supplied office equipment stores. If you are like me, too tight to spend five dollars on a fancy book, you can make one up for about ten cents with a plain piece of paper and a ruler. You know how you function. Trying to adapt your budget to a fancy accounting system at this point may be too discouraging.

The budget samples on pages 114-115 are suggestions you may wish to follow in your own budget program. Look them over and then modify or expand them to meet your own situation.

WHERE THERE'S A WILL

Another area we should discuss relative to the money game is the need for the single to settle his own personal estate by making out a will. It continually amazes me that many individuals fail to see the necessity of this legal document. I've heard people say, "My parents will take care of the kids," or "My sister and I have made arrangements to look after one another's family if anything happens to either of us."

Not so! It is up to the state in which you reside to make that judgment.

If you have a will and spell out your desires in it, the state will then carry out *your* wishes.

If you are single and have no former marriage partner, you may ask, "Why bother?" But you still should have a will. You have life insurance, personal belongings, your automobile (which, if under a finance plan is insuring your life), and your loving dog or cat. If you have brothers or sisters or an elderly parent, you may very much want to provide something for them in the event something happens to you. You may wish to set up a trust fund to educate a niece or nephew in the years to come. If you do *not* have a will, *none of your wishes will be carried out.*

In my own case, after my first wife's death, I had a living trust drawn up for the children. This instrument provided that all my assets upon death were to go into a trust, and the trustees, whom I selected, would handle the care and distribution of funds according to the needs of my surviving children. I also would let the trustees care for me in the event I became mentally or physically incapable of handling my own affairs.

Now I complicated things by marrying a second time. What happened to the trust? It was simply amended to include June as the primary person and to provide for the children should both of us be killed at the same time.

I have found that a bank with a good trust department can provide valuable counseling for you in your estate planning. A bank's main purpose is to handle money, and that is what you are asking them to do for you.

If you have life insurance in effect, ask your agent to come over and review your situation. You should especially do this if you have lost your partner through death or divorce. In some instances, a sharp agent will contact *you.* I can gladly say that my own insurance agent was at my side within hours of my wife's death, and he and his family did so much to help us that I can never even that score, no matter how much or little insurance I buy.

DON'T COUNT ON IT

If you have been recently divorced and have arranged a settlement for child support or alimony, do not rest too strongly on the continual payment of that support. We have discovered that after two or three years, most alimony and child support payments are no longer made. The courts are so busy divorcing people that they do not have time to enforce former orders, and very few judges are willing to lock up a former husband for lack of support.

We have learned that the best step to take, if at all possible, is to begin a new direction in your life and to realize that you will have to support yourself and your youngsters. In most cases, you will be able to "retool" and get established within a few years. You may not be able to enjoy the same standard of living you did previously, but you *will* live and have the dignity and self-respect that comes when you make it on your own.

One of the women in our singles group took over nine months to recover from the initial shock of her husband's leaving her. She could not face the thought of working on a regular basis. After two or three months of counseling, she agreed to work part-time in a hospital for one summer. By the end of her three-month stay, she had built several new relationships and found that her hurt was beginning to heal. When fall came, we encouraged her to try full-time employment. She was hired by a local firm and is now doing quite nicely. When she first talked with us, she was barely able to make it through a day. Now, through the love, prayers, and support of many Christian friends, she has passed through this period of fear and doubt and has a new confidence and a new self-image.

A final tip: Don't get caught up in the stock market if you can't afford to lose your money! And if you feel you *can* afford to lose some, be sure you contact a reputable broker before becoming involved.

Money can be a disrupting factor for the single person. If you have not yet encountered a financial crisis, take advantage of good planning practices to avoid that possibility. If you are feeling a burden in this area, share your problem with a trusted friend and pray together for God to give you support and wisdom to see beyond today's bills.

Then seek out competent financial counseling. As you look for solutions to your money problems, look to people:

1. you *trust*
2. who *understand* your situation, and
3. who will act in *your best interest.*

THE
FUTURE

NINE
BURNING EMBERS
(Bob)

IT WAS A COOL EVENING, and I built a fire in our living room fireplace. June and I figured it would add some warmth to our souls as well as our bodies while we were getting to know our expected guests. This would be the first meeting of a group trying to put something together to help formerly married singles.

By the time the fire was glowing with crimson embers dropping through the grate, some five people had arrived. We all had one thing in common. This was our first meeting, and most were scared. Who was this couple opening up their home to meet with divorcees, widows, and widowers, they wondered. Quite frankly, we were scared, too. This was a new experience for us as well.

As in most any group, the conversation was guarded and rather sparing. Seven of us were now sipping coffee and eating the goodies prepared for the evening. One at a time, the guests began to relate why they had come and what they hoped to find in a Christian singles group. As the night progressed, people relaxed and conversation became more free. By the end of the evening, it was the consensus of opinion that we should try to meet at least once a month to talk and have an informal program.

June and I began to discuss the meeting and the possible future of the group as we cleaned up the kitchen. We could see some ten or fifteen people coming each month for some good clean fun and sharing as they sought to put their lives back together again. We were confident that our home was adequate to host such a group for a long time to come.

As I write this nearly three years later, more than 500 people have come to our home for some kind of Singles function. We do not advertise, except through our monthly newsletter, The Soloist. We have tried not to put an emphasis on numbers, nor have we formally kept count of those who attended our get-togethers. But now we average anywhere from fifty to ninety persons a month.

We quickly realized that we needed competent, professional assistance to handle a work of this magnitude. We asked for help from our local Christian community and formed an advisory board. As a result, we have been able to offer many quality programs with professional leadership from all walks of life. We have dealt with loneliness, finances, the sex drive, and other "heavy" issues. And we have had potluck suppers, Thanksgiving dinners, and open house nights, as well.

The fact that so many people within the Christian community are wrestling with the whole issue of being single (either never-married or formerly married singleness) has made us prayerfully consider the future of our group.

We know that if 500 people have responded to our very minor efforts, there must be thousands (both within and without the church) who are seeking support and guidance in their single state.

Starting that evening in our living room with those first five members, we learned that singles have many different problems. Not one program or emphasis could meet all the needs of all the people. One need, however, was prevalent; that was the need to be able to relax and to laugh—with no obligations. Contrary to the routine in a singles' bar, the evening's entertainment for us does *not* end in a motel room! This fact became the glue that held our group together. People wanted to be interested in each other's needs and experiences, with no sexual obligation.

We began to structure our meetings to include a social time regardless of the formal program. It has been most interesting to observe a group of forty, fifty, or sixty people, some of whom have never met before, talking freely with one another. In the course of an evening, small groups can be seen in various sections of the living room, dining room, kitchen, or den, all functioning in a different manner. One group might be laughing uproariously, while another might be immersed in extremely serious conversation. Others would be chatting about the speaker's comments.

Once we found that the greatest needs were fellowship and friendship, we were able to see that some personal doors that had been sealed tight because of mistrust and hurt were beginning to open.

When a person comes into the group and feels free because there is no price to pay for being present, he learns not only to relax but to begin that all-important step toward rebuilding trust relationships.

Perhaps divorced men and women are especially low on trust, but the widowed individual as well needs to have trust rebuilt after everything he had confidence in has been crushed by death. In my own experience, trusting God to be Lord of my life after my first wife's death was most difficult. I wanted to blame God for my great loss and therefore asked whether I could trust a God who would willfully hurt me so much.

For the never-married single, trust is also a major issue. Our society has come to realize that the single community has become a great economic force, much like our marketing pros have focused on the teenage marketplace for so many years. Singles' bars, cruises, weekends, and other "specials" are aimed at this group. Not all these are rip-offs, but most promise far more than they deliver.

The church has not helped that trust level to rise too much, because in its own way, the church, too, has exploited the single. Intentionally or not, the church has been guilty of saying to the single, in effect, "You have the *time* to teach Sunday school," while it has not allowed the single to hold other leadership positions because of his single status. Neither has the church sought to meet the single's specific needs.

It took about a year before people invested their trust in our Christian Singles Foundation. We always have what we call the "shoppers"—those who are looking to find some action. They come occasionally to our meetings, but they soon see that shopping is not the name of the game. One year two such men came to our Christmas party. Both of them tried for an hour to pick up some of the very nice young ladies present. Even our son Steve who was pouring punch, noticed what was going on and later said to me, "Boy, I've never heard a guy put down so fast in my life!" Needless to say, within a short time the shoppers were on their way to more productive territory.

Fellowship and trust are topics that go well with whipped cream and cherries, but there are times when a single's needs are much deeper and are on a very practical level. We soon learned that some of our single friends needed assistance in areas of housing, employment, legal aid, food, and clothing.

Last Christmas was a perfect example of the practical work that can be done by a singles' ministry. One of our group learned that another person was in a terrible financial bind. Christmas was coming, bills were piling up, and she was fearful that her electricity and heat supply would be cut off. Word was out that daddy was coming on Christmas with his arms loaded with gifts for the children he seldom visited during the year. The emotional strain on this woman was too much. How could she have a decent Christmas with no food, no heat, a pile of bills, and her ex-Santa arriving for his annual pilgrimage?

Without any names being used, a small group did some telephoning to other friends and raised $200 in cash. The woman was presented with the cash and some personal gifts for herself by two representatives of the larger body of believers. It was a thrilling experience for us to participate together in a love gift like this, and it was equally thrilling for our friend to have the privilege of receiving such love.

Most of the ideas for our group activities and speakers have come right from our members. We are very fortunate in our location, as we have a seminary, college, counseling center, and the Evangelistic Association of New England within a telephone call for our resources.

Two Christian psychologists have used our group as a reentry step for many of their clients who have come through a death or divorce experience.

One ministry we have just begun to explore is in helping the children of divorced parents. We were reminded of the needs of children who have one parent absent when we had an all-day outing at the Cathedral-in-the-Pines in New Hampshire. We chartered a bus for the ninety-mile trip. As soon as the bus was underway and the ice was broken with the children, one little girl came over and sat in my lap for the entire trip. On the way home I had *two* lap-fillers! I noticed our son Jim, who was 16 at the time, had two or three of the smaller children all over him. The children who lived in a male-absent home responded to the attention and touch of love they received from a man. We noticed the same was true in the lives of the children being raised by their dads.

Where are we in our dreams and plans with the Christian Singles Foundation? We dream of one day having a residence that will be available for any single who needs to get away. There will be several people there who love and care, and who will be able to talk, to counsel, to help heal the wounds of heartbreak and grief.

It will be a home in which there is room and time to linger over coffee or to retreat for study. There will be teaching from Scripture; there will be peace.

There will be miles to walk, perhaps an ocean view to lose oneself in. There will be professional counseling available if it is needed. It will be a place of beginning again.

We have rewritten the 23rd Psalm for the single whom Jesus loves. It is our prayer that this psalm will become a reality for those going through a death or divorce:

The Lord is my Shepherd, I have learned to trust again.
He has helped me to lie down and to be content in my single state.
He is leading me into new waters of calmness and peace.
He has restored my soul, which was broken and rejected.
He is helping me to find those new paths of righteousness that I believed did not exist.

I have learned through all my hurts, not to fear any longer.
He alone is my peace and my stability.
He has taught me to love myself again, because he loves me.
He has healed the pain, and I am full of joy because I know he is all I need.

I have had a grievous time thus far, but he has shown me that
days ahead are not for me to be alone. He is near.
One day I know that I will see him and be pleased to have walked
this path, which leads to his eternal home.

As our ministry continues to grow, we experience some
fears and uncertainties about the future. We have seen other
Christians begin para-church ministries with God's blessing,
only to end up fighting the church and its people at every
turn. That, of course, is the last thing we want, and we are
continually seeking out ways to work with our local churches
and be an extension of them.

As we write this chapter, once again we are sitting in a room
watching the crimson glow from burning embers. The night is
cool, the fire warm. In two more years, what will have come
from our vision?

TEN

UNLOCKING THE DOOR
(Bob)

OUR PRESENT HOUSE HAS A VERY UNUSUAL FEATURE: two front doors. This confused us, as well as our visitors, until I learned that the owner and builder of the house had screens on the front porch. He used one door as a direct access to the house and the other as an access to the front porch.

It was obvious to us that the former owner seldom used the door that had led to the screened porch. As a result of layer after layer of paint and years of expansion from the humid weather, it became stuck. Rather than go through a major repair situation, I decided to leave the door sealed tight.

Last year I hired a strong young seminary student to paint my house. One evening after returning from work, I found the "sealed" door open and my young friend painting it.

"How in the world did you get that door open?" I asked.

He looked at me with a bewildered stare and answered, "Wasn't it supposed to be opened? I just put my shoulder to it and pushed."

For many years the church has been saying to the single person (especially to the formerly married), "We have a door that is locked. It would be great if we could find a way to open it, because then you could quietly come into our services and not cause too much unrest."

It is just within the past few years that some churches have had someone putting their shoulder to the sealed door to bang it open. What they have found is that the people using that formerly sealed door are no different in terms of needs, fears, and desires than those who have been using the standard door all these years. A formerly married Christian is a formerly married member of a Christian couple.

One of the major roadblocks to accepting the formerly married person in the church is the whole issue of divorce and remarriage. For many years, the church has been like a hospital that refused to treat a patient for a broken arm because he might have been exposed to smallpox the week before.

People who have genuinely turned to the church for help have found, in a majority of congregations, a cold, indifferent body of people who are fearful of what disease could spread into their sterile community by this hurting, formerly married, person.

In most of our conservative churches the issue seems to be, may a divorced person remarry? What has been lost in this issue is that the divorced person is coming to the church and to its leadership in order that his or her needs may be met, not to get married.

A few years ago, I had a business associate who was divorced. She had been brought up to attend church regularly. As she attempted to establish a new life, she began

131

attending a new church. For more than a year she and her three-year-old daughter went every week. One day, she invited a male friend to join her. For the first time in more than a year, she was recognized with lines such as "Welcome. Are you a new family in the area?"

"I went seeking spiritual strength and fellowship," she told me. "But it was not until I conformed to the family image of a man, woman, and child, that people in the church seemed interested in who I was, or cared to get to know me. I left and never went back."

One of the fears in the church is that the formerly married's status is "catching," or that his person will lead someone in the church astray. More and more the single—especially the formerly married—finds that he (or she) is a threat to the married community.

Most of the formerly married persons whom we have met admit that the last thing on their minds when they attend church and church functions is marriage. They are going to have their emotional and spiritual needs met. When a person has been married five, ten, or twenty years and then finds himself suddenly alone with no one to communicate with except the cat or bird, the church should be an ideal place to come to have fellowship with others.

During the past two years we have begun to see the locked doors being opened. When we first started Christian Singles Foundation, only a few ministers in the area encouraged and supported us. Within the past year, however, many more churches have opened their doors to programs designed to meet the needs of singles.

Recently we were asked, "Why do singles' ministries differ from other ministries in the church?" The following is a list of some of the answers we came up with:

1. *The church has viewed itself as a married institution for centuries and has viewed the single as abnormal.*

Right away I can hear some of you saying how many Sunday school teachers are single, that the Junior-high leader is single, and the Sunday soloist is single. I view these as service positions to the marriage-unit philosophy of the church. The marriage-unit philosophy is not wrong in itself; it is wrong when the unit begins to exploit the single person in order to have its needs met without considering the needs of the single persons involved in that service.

The issue here is very much the same issue as integration was back in the 1950s. The black person not only wanted the privilege to work for XYZ Corporation, but he wanted the opportunity to become a leader and possible owner of XYZ. The right of being equal was being denied the black members of our society by our green line of discrimination called money power.

For the single in the church, the issue has become one of how the single can make a meaningful contribution and will the single be accepted in the circle of leadership and authority, even if he does not have a wedding ring?

Let us add that we believe the church has a responsibility to teach and hold up to new heights the sacrament of marriage. Marriage within the church could become one of the strongest Christian witnesses to the secular society's emphasis on free love. But for too many years, *marriage* has been the goal of the Christian community rather than the *building up of persons* to establish themselves as individual believers who may or may not choose to be married.

2. Christians have felt that marriage is the will of God for everybody.

Recently my wife and I had a conversation with a minister's wife who was always trying to match this woman with that man, knowing she had found "just the right person" for each of them. After much discussion, we finally asked her, "Why do you feel it necessary to find a mate for every single? Is it necessary to marry them off in order to assure them happiness?"

Suddenly, as if someone had turned on a light, she said, "You know, I have never thought that a person could be happy as a single; I guess because marriage has always been the ultimate in fulfillment for me."

For many years we have been taught that Missionary X was called to be single, or Brother Y had such a marvelous ministry because he was willing to forsake all and devote himself to his calling. In light of what is developing in our society today and in our churches, I would urge all ministers to be sure the people they are marrying have that same sense of call to their lives together as husband and wife.

We were told recently about a minister who counseled a friend by saying it was "God's will for everyone to be married." We could not believe such counsel, especially after viewing some of the marriage failures we have seen over the past few years.

I do believe marriage is God's plan so that men and women may live together and share their lives; but to say boldly that marriage is the will of God for everyone is neither true nor scriptural. If such a statement were true, then Jesus Christ was living out of the will of God.

3. Our entire western culture holds marriage as the ultimate fulfillment in life.

Unfortunately, the church has adopted much of our culture's teachings about marriage and its meaning, and the media teaches us that marriage has been replaced by sex to provide fulfillment.

If a person is a miserable single, getting married (or having sexual relationships) will not produce anything but a miserable married person. Contentment is God's gift. Learning to be content is a gift of God's grace. Knowing yourself and loving the person you are is far more important than conforming to any societal pressure or clerical imposition. Contentment comes from knowing the heart of God, finding that daily revelation of his peace through the Prince of Peace, Jesus Christ.

4. The single person is a threat to the average marriage.

This is not only an accusation, it is a fact. Our society assumes the single life is not acceptable; therefore, everyone must be looking for a mate—*but don't you take mine!*

The image of the swinging single is being proven false more and more. Singles are not usually interested in breaking up couples for the sake of finding a marriage partner for themselves. The average single faces the pressure of finances, career, housing, parents, and he knows marriage is *not* the automatic solution to them.

I do not have statistics to prove my statement, but I firmly believe most marriages are broken by infidelity and that the majority of those infidelities are between two married persons, not between a married and a single person who is content to remain single.

5. The church has not learned how to work with and for the needs of single persons in the same way it has learned to work with other aspects of the church family, e.g., youth, family, the elderly.

Recognizing that the vast majority of its leadership is married and has very little experience in dealing with the single life, the church finds itself wanting in this area of ministry. In the late 50s the campus became the focal point of parachurch ministries. The most fruitful ministry in several generations arose from the effort of such groups as Inter-Varsity, Campus Crusade, and other well-known student works. Today there are missionaries all over the world because of the special challenge given to students.

If the church is going to have an impact on the single

community, it must learn from such specialized ministries. It must rely on people who live in the single world and who know the hurts and bitterness of loneliness, broken relationships, and unresponsive church leadership. In the 70s, we need more churches, denominations, and Christian leaders who are willing to invest their time, money, and lives in the ministry of singles if the church is going to make headway against the tide of free love and marriage-less units.

6. Singles come in various forms (never-married, widowed, divorced, separated) with different needs at different times.

As a former youth worker in the church, I can look back and realize that although their situations might be different and their habits might vary, most teenagers are alike. Working with teens in New York's Hell's Kitchen was not too different from working with teens from affluent Fort Lauderdale.

Entering into a singles' ministry, however, introduces you to people of all needs, backgrounds, economic levels, and personal experiences. Some are working through the death of a beloved partner; others are working through bitterness, hate, and anger fired by divorce. Others are shattered by the walkout of a partner and cannot face themselves in the mirror because of a poor self-image. Single parents face the perplexities of trying to be both parents to their children, of working to support the family, of making ends meet financially.

Several churches in America have begun extremely effective work with singles and have multiskilled staff to help meet the needs of the person alone.

There was a time when being single meant just that . . . single and never married. Now when a person says he or she is single, our minds run through a series of questions. Is he separated? Divorced? If so, we wonder and ask each other if it was a bloody, knock-down battle, an amicable separation, or a case of infidelity on one partner's part.

In the church, the single who has been married is almost compelled to explain his status in order to receive acceptance. Our plea here is to ask the church to open its doors to the single as a *person,* not as a *category.*

7. The church has put its theology before the needs of the single, often acting as a judge before the facts have been heard.

A young lady was left alone after her husband walked out on her and his son. For seven years the woman waited. She was a faithful member of her church, attending regularly and serving in a limited role because of her working schedule and her family obligations.

After seven years, the woman had her husband declared legally dead. One year after that, she remarried.

The church was bitterly divided over the issue of whether or not it would be right for her to be married in the sanctuary. In all the debate over theology, not one individual took time to treat the woman or her family decently, or to remember her faithfulness to the church and to the Lord for nearly eight years.

Recently I was chatting with a theology professor of an evangelical seminary about this issue. He made a statement that shocked me. "I do not believe there is one word of Scripture directed to the person who is divorced," he said. "There is much written *about* divorce, but to my understanding, the divorced person does not have one word of Holy Scripture specifically directed *at* him. Surely there are admonitions that apply, but these words apply to *all* people."

8. Many pastors do not have the skills or the freedom to gain the skills of working with singles, sometimes because of the restrictions of parish politics.

This one is not going to win us many friends, but as we have traveled in our limited circle of the singles ministry, we have heard pastor after pastor confess his helplessness in a ministry for singles.

Many pastors have become competent in marriage and grief counseling, but dealing with the single has had a low priority. The basic reason is that most ministers were married before, during, or right after seminary. They do not remember what it is like to be single and therefore have never viewed singles as a group of people who could use a separate emphasis within the church structure.

When talking with friends who are in full-time ministry, some have openly confided their desire to begin a work in this area but have found the power structure of the church against them.

Unfortunately, power structures *do* exist in churches. The divorced person is one who is misunderstood and often suspect. For this reason many church leaders will not permit the pastoral staff to engage in a "controversial" kind of ministry. We heard Dr. Kenneth Chafin of South Main Baptist Church in Houston, Texas, once tell a group of listeners, all of whom were in some kind of church ministry, not to start a singles ministry unless the entire church family understood the needs of the single and was willing to support the work. Dr. Chafin knows whereof he speaks. He has one of the strongest singles ministries in the nation.

9. The church, for the most part, is out of touch with the singles world.

It is interesting to note that when a family invites a single person to dinner, they often think it necessary to arrange for a second single to be present. More often than not, of course, the second single will be a member of the opposite sex.

The church as a whole has misconceptions about the lives single people lead. The idea is that they have more time to devote to church work (which is true for some, but not true for many others), more money to contribute, more energy to invest. But like anyone else, the single needs to earn a living, care for an apartment or home, and look after family members—without the support of a partner.

We need to learn from the single persons in our midst, what *they* need and want from the local Body of Christ with whom they minister.

During the past few months, we have been attending a downtown Boston church in which we agreed to assist with a singles' work they have begun. One Sunday, a young lady from California came to the group for the first time. We discovered her to be a delightful young woman on a professional internship in the Boston area.

As a result of the group's activities, we had her, along with some thirty others, to our home for a New Year's Eve hay ride. After an hour's journey through the frozen backwoods of New England, the group came to our house. During the course of the evening, this young woman became friends with June's mother, who lives with us. Before the night was over she and Mom had become the best of buddies and, upon leaving the house sometime near 2:00 A.M., she commented to us that it was certainly good to be in a home again.

For many of us who have homes and families, we forget that those who are in transitional stages of their lives do not have homes in which there is warmth, security, and the attention of older people.

HOW CAN THE CHURCH RESPOND?

A good place to begin is to start looking around at what you have that can be shared with others. We sometimes become too program-conscious and think we need a series of "hit" activities each week or that we need Ph.D's or other magnetic types of people as leaders. We firmly believe that the local church can begin a group with one interested, committed couple who is willing to share their lives, their home, their children, and their grandparents with others.

At a seminar June and I recently held, a minister's wife came to see us about starting a group. She and her husband knew of our work and were interested in learning more. We surprised her by saying we did not feel that she and her husband, as the pastor and wife, should start the singles' group alone. We believe the politics in a small congregation can be so great that if the pastor led the group, it could interfere with his other ministries.

We urged her to find a mature couple with an outwardly good marriage to lead the group. They should be a couple who are willing to learn the needs of singles, willing to listen to them, and willing to pray about their part in such an important church role. Once convinced that this is an area where they can be of service to the Lord, then the ministry can begin.

If at all possible, do not bring the group into the church setting on the first night. The more homey and warm you can make it, the better you will find the response. This statement may upset a few ministers who feel that most activities should be held within the physical confines of the church, and we personally know of one growing group that does, indeed, meet within the church structure. But this is a large church with a multiple staff.

If you are thinking of starting a work, we strongly suggest you visit a work that is currently going on. June and I were privileged to visit South Main Baptist Church in Houston on two separate occasions. We learned a great deal from their material, but we learned more by just talking with people involved in that ministry.

What do we do in our Christian singles' group? We have found that the most helpful programs come from our own people as they respond to their needs. We often ask what kinds of programs those in our group are interested in having, and in the three years we have been meeting, only one such program has really bombed. Most deal with the current questions those in the group are wrestling with: financial situations, sexual behavior for the Christian, loneliness, how to use one's creativity, etc.

Whenever possible, we seek to have professionals to handle a topic, but this is not always necessary. What *is* necessary is to have speakers who *know* their subject, can articulate it, and can be open to those they are addressing.

How do you spread the word about your new singles' ministry? Put a notice in church bulletins throughout your town, a blurb in the local newspaper, or send out a well-done (not necessarily expensive) newsletter listing activities.

Recently June was interviewed on one of Boston's leading news radio stations. They had found our names in a brochure citing a seminar entitled "Beginning Again" that we were leading, and they were curious because they didn't realize that "religion" was also in the singles business! Well, we assured them that Christ was in the business and, therefore, so were we.

What was the result? Our telephone started ringing with friends saying they had heard the broadcast, and before long a few very shy voices began calling saying that they had listened to the program and were interested in attending our meetings.

Opening the door for the single person means meeting their needs. We fully agree that many of the needs deal with spiritual concerns, but not all singles will come for such a program. We have found that a balanced program of fun, good food, and instruction as to the "hows" of beginning again, dealing with the single life, and how to be a friend to yourself will find great acceptance.

One word of caution must be raised about those in leadership with such a group—especially if the group involves formerly married people. If a man and woman are having problems in the area of controlling their own sexual desires, *they should not get involved in the leadership.* Too many Christians have found their ministry ruined by this issue. Leaders for a singles' ministry—or any kind of ministry—must be mature. Our definition of *mature* is that a person can handle his or her own problems and not become involved in the problems of others to the point of self-destruction.

All of the meetings and counseling sessions should be done on neutral ground, with a husband or wife within a polite radius. Often women will want to talk to a man or vice versa, and that is fine. We will invite someone to our home, and if they have special requests, one of us will go to another room so that the visitor can have a confidential *but not isolated* chat.

Many psychologists and psychiatrists advocate "touch" sessions. This may be fine for some persons, but we strongly urge that such an activity in the setting of the formerly married is extremely dangerous. Some of the men and women who come to our home have obvious physical needs. They are attractive, warm people, and many have become good friends with whom we share a hug of friendship from time to time. But the dangers of physical contact need to be upheld in our day. June and I smiled when we heard a pastor recently tell a large group of people that in their church, where affection and love abounds, "We stress giving *side* hugs, because I personally find that those front hugs can become un-spiritual!" Good advice!

How can we stress here the subtlety that exists in relationships today without conveying to you, the reader, a paranoia? Perhaps a "holy" paranoia *should* exist to some extent. Our heads continue to reel as we hear of Christian psychologists, pastors, youth workers, etc., who become embroiled in physical liaisons—innocent at first, but growing less and less innocent physically, spiritually, and emotionally as the relationship progresses. It's time we Christians clean up our morals, mentally and physically. This is a warning the church needs to issue to its own repeatedly because of the culture in which we live.

DEVELOPING A SINGLES MINISTRY

Perhaps you have read this chapter and are saying to yourself, "All this is fine, but I really do not know where to begin. I have no radio interviews, no psychologists to ask for help, and no mature couple in my church who seem interested in being involved with singles."

If you are a minister, use your congregation's knowledge about singles in your community. If you are a lay couple interested in helping, speak to friends about the need. Here are a few ideas you might like to consider:

● Look within your own congregation. Your people will be able to identify six to ten friends of theirs who would like to have some form of wholesome activities designed to meet the needs of singles. Do a formal survey if you wish, for two or three Sundays, as an outreach program. Don't convey the impression that the singles are your new mission project. Rather, let them know you are interested in them as individuals and that you recognize that the church has ignored them for too long.

● Place a small ad in the local newspaper with a telephone number for people to call for more information. We have seen ads that read:

> SINGLES AND FORMERLY MARRIEDS
> New friendship and fun group forming to meet once a week. If you are tired of the bars, the exploitation, and the singles' stigma, why not give us a call? 555-1212.

● Make a few posters to place in grocery stores, barber

shops, and banks. Make them look as handsome as possible, but not professional in the sense that they look like they are an extension of a national franchise out to exploit the single.

- Call the local newspaper editor and tell him or her of your plans, giving the time and place of the first meeting.
- Send handwritten notes to individuals whom you know, or who have come to your attention, because they have recently gone through a divorce or separation. Invite them to come.
- Hold the meetings on a neutral ground. Your church building may be beautiful, but your church image may not be as attractive to the single who has been made to feel guilty because of his/her "sin" of divorce.
- Make sure there are some people to act as hosts and hostesses for the first few meetings, even offering to give rides to people who call.
- Do not give the sermon you love most at your first meeting! What people are looking for at this time is a new friend, a smiling face, their first laugh in a couple years (if they have recently gone through the death of a loved one or the death of a marriage), and yes, a place in which they can feel free to cry if necessary.
- If you believe your church is too small and you cannot handle the concept of a singles' group alone, join hands with a sister church or two. Our beginning grew out of one church and the personal letters written by the pastor to several of his friends in the area.
- If you are a pastor, include singles in your pastoral prayer each week. June remembers listening to ministers pray for the children, the college students, the elderly, and the missionaries for years, while a large number of singles in the congregation were never mentioned. If you include singles this way, the sincerity of your interest in them will be seen and recognized by those who are alone in your congregation.
- Pray. Now I probably sound like the minister who

realizes that all else has failed, but I am serious. Until the single person becomes a part of your prayer life and your conversation, you will just be running another function and will not be developing a burden that God has put before you. We know of a church in which the pastor has said in no uncertain terms, "Our church is not capable of dealing with the problems of singles, and we do not make an attempt, therefore, to even begin a ministry with them."

Does that sound like Jesus as he wept over Jerusalem or when he met the woman at the well? Did he put her down for being single and formerly married? That question may sound sarcastic; if so, forgive me. But we limit God so much by our lack of confidence in what we can do or what our church can do. It may be time for you to listen to what God wants you to do for the people around you in the pews of your church.

● If you are a pastor, preach a series of sermons on the contemporary problems of our society. Some ideas:

Is marriage going to survive in our society?

Who cleans up after the divorce?

Trends in our society . . . are they biblical or satanic?

How to build and preserve your marriage.

Why was Jesus Christ single? (If God chose a woman to conceive his Son, why didn't he give him a mate?)

For the pastors using titles like these, or who seek to develop their own, let me warn you that you will not find a great amount of material on singles today, although more and more is being written. Here is an opportunity for you to do some real digging and to make a contribution of your own.

● We believe that the church needs to start teaching the biblical view of sexual relationships and sexual intercourse below the junior- and senior-high levels as well as to the adults.

We have attended conferences at which sexual subjects have been part of the program but have been described as "For Couples Only." But if young people are going to understand the biblical view of their sex life, then singles need to be welcomed into such discussions. Healthy family units can lend a hand to those that are broken; pastors and church workers can be sensitive to the needs of children in one-parent homes. Of course, the formerly married head of household has to make his family's needs known. The church must help heal the broken family.

● Finally, the church must begin a whole new emphasis on personal purity. This means not only speaking from the pulpit about biblical moral standards but demonstrating in our own lives that we take God's moral order seriously. Most important, we need to learn how to do this with no sense of being censorious but with a positive affirmation of all that is good.

In reviewing much of this chapter, we realize we have come down heavily on the church. This by no means says we think the church is not capable of ministering to single adults. It is. Our plea here is for those of us who are married to take the time to look at the singles in our midst as individuals who are worthy to be known, and to realize that there is much we can learn from them.

Singles, put your shoulders to the unlocked doors with us and push! Help us to know who you are. And understand us, as we would seek to understand you.

HOPE

ELEVEN

JESUS WAS A SINGLE ADULT
(June)

HAVE YOU EVER THOUGHT OF HIM that way? As a single . . . as one who went through life with friends, but not with a wife and children? As one who knew what it was to care for an elderly parent? As one who was thought of as different? As one who had to relax in other people's homes? As one who cried alone in a garden when not one other person could understand his grief? As one who, in spite of his aloneness, had a purpose, a drive, an excitement, a goal, a talent to share? One who knew who he was, what he was doing, where he was going, and who was willing to be the person he was—with all its strife, hurt, misunderstanding, and glory?

Jesus was a single adult.

Through the four Gospels, we can look at Jesus as a man,

as well as God, and see the way he related to others. What was important to him? Who was important to him? How did he compensate for the things he *didn't* have . . . a permanent home, a family of his own . . . and how did he respond to fear and loneliness?

JESUS MADE A FAMILY

Although not part of a husband/wife relationship, Jesus did have a family. Not sired by a human father, he still matured and grew in a family setting, having brothers and sisters. Once he reached the point of independence from those relationships, he still cared for his widowed mother and slowly made a family of his own. The small band of men he gathered around him became those with whom he lived.

In the Gospels, we see that he taught his followers and discipled them. He kept pressing home truths to that little group. In his relationships with them, there was the spirit of human fellowship and emotions as well as a spiritual quality.

In John we read the shortest verse in Scripture, "Jesus wept." If he wept, somehow we feel he must have laughed as well. When friends come to our home for a meal, there are sometimes serious discussions, but often there are joyous, laughing times, and so it must have been for Jesus. One gets the feeling after reading of the Lord's visits to the home of Mary, Martha, and Lazarus that he enjoyed the fellowship there. Surely there must have been times when they were not engrossed in heavy conversation but just enjoyed recalling the day's activities. By this we do not mean to say Jesus was less than he was—Holy Son of Holy Father—but there was a human side to him as well, and that human part of Jesus had human characteristics.

The family he made—his disciples and friends—were those with whom he could talk and share. They surely could not fully understand him, but he was someone they could relate to, and he was someone who cared about them and made that caring obvious. They did not have to wonder if his mood were touchy or if they should cloak their inner feelings at any moment. They knew him to be a stable person in whom they could confide, someone who understood them and the pressures they faced. He was approachable, a friend who could give them the help they needed at any time.

JESUS AND LIFE

None of us is immune to the questions of personal self-image, loneliness, or fear. Jesus was constantly called on to account for his authority and in one way or another, to say who he was. What is impressive is that Jesus did know who he was and everything he did was done in character.

As Christians, we need to realize that if that were true for Christ during his earthly ministry, it is true for us as well. Do I doubt he is Savior? Lord? That he has a plan for me and for this world? That he taught me truths that *are* truths, and that those truths do not change because of the world's opinion of them? Can I say I know who I am with the same kind of assurance he did? I can if I trust his word.

Our problem is that we like to be part of the world as well as to partake of the good things Jesus offers us. The problem then becomes, Which will I choose? My feelings of insecurity or poor self-image come from my desire to conform to the world around me or to my *self* instead of to him. This is easy to say but difficult to change. I have to decide to which audience I will play: to the Lord and his heavenly galaxy or to my peers?

HE KNOWS LONELINESS

What is more lonely than being with someone close by and knowing that that person is completely unaware of your inside turmoil? Peter stood before Christ and told him he would never let him down. Jesus stared back sadly, knowing fear would make this friend shout, "I never knew him! I'm *not* one of his followers!"

Crying with a broken heart in the garden, Christ tried numerous times to rouse his friends out of their sleep so they could give him the support he needed. Each time he returned to their side, he found they had dozed again. "Can't you watch with me just one hour?" he asked with desperation. Looking into his face, they could not understand his grief. Jesus was lonely.

HE KNOWS FEAR

"Father, if it be your will, let this cup pass from me." He audibly cried in his anguish. He desperately sought to change the circumstances he was facing. But knowing the father did not necessarily mean that hurt would be taken away or that he could retreat from the road he had been destined to walk. There was a divine purpose, a divine plan, and he was the center of it all. Would he walk the whole way, or would he turn back? Would he accept the Father's view of being a king, or would he succumb to the crowd's? Scholars may debate whether indeed Christ *could* have turned his back on his Father, but I wonder if he could not have let the fear pull him away.

The tension of that night in the Garden of Gethsemane won the ultimate victory for mankind. Is there a victory for me to win, too?

JESUS AND SECURITY

Nothing seems to be as intimidating as feeling insecure. Finances lend a certain security to life. People lend a certain security. Routine lends a certain security. But what happens when they are ripped away? What happens when the money is gone, the job over? Jesus found he couldn't find his security in his friends, in his family, in his credibility as a teacher, in *anything* but the Father. Perhaps this is the greatest lesson we can learn from his early example: security must ultimately be only to him. Only *he* knows the total picture of what makes us who and what we are; only he can be trusted to be there when everything and everyone falls out of our lives.

JESUS WAS A SEXUAL BEING

The first time I heard that statement I nearly fell out of my pew. I thought Jesus was being degraded in some way, until it was explained that he did not feel uncomfortable in the presence of women and he did not shy away from them. He was one who enjoyed their company, as is evidenced by his visits to the home of Mary and Martha and their brother Lazarus. Mary Magdelene followed him; so did other women—not to lust after Jesus, as some would seek to infer, but to learn the truths of life he taught. He in turn needed their wholesome love and concern, gifts given to them to share.

Have you ever thought of Jesus as a single adult?

Have you ever looked at the experiences—the *human* experiences—he lived through and seen some area with which you could identify?

He has been happy; he has been rejected; he has been laughed at and made out to be a fool. He has known the responsibility of caring for a parent and providing for her care for when he would no longer be physically present. He has lost a friend to death and known the need to weep. He has felt, and been, alone. He has experienced fear. He has lived this life and known the ground we tread.

He has been tempted and not given in; he has loved with a true love and has known what it is to accept love in return. He has traveled for days without a place to lay his head. He has experienced the entire scope of emotions available.

He has been sick and in pain. He has been physically abused. He has walked the beach and climbed the hillside. He has played with children and held them close. They were not his, and yet they were, because his love made them his. He has talked with the politician and sparred with the priest.

153

JESUS WAS A SINGLE ADULT

He has lost his temper and he has hammered a nail. He has cooked a dinner and shared it with others. He has known the palace and he has known the cross.

Look at him, this Jesus . . . this Jesus who was a single adult. Look at him and make him the model for your single life. Look at him and start to live.

JESUS IN SCRIPTURE

Jesus can identify with our emotions and needs. Looking at Jesus as a man, and remembering his God-nature at the same time, helps us remember the strength and help he can give us in our daily lives.

MAN WITH A PAST
Read Luke 1—2.
Where was Mary when she learned that the coming of Christ would be through her own body? Was anyone with her?

Note Mary's response (Luke 1: 46-55) and compare it with Joseph's when he learned of Mary's condition (Matt. 1: 19). What were Joseph's initial plans?

How were those plans changed (Matt. 1: 20-25)?

Describe how you think this background could have made Jesus' ministry difficult at first (Read Luke 4: 14-30).

What is there in your own past that other people do not fully understand or that *looks* questionable (whether it is or not)?

What was Jesus' attitude toward those who saw him only as a hometown boy and not as the teacher he was?

Does this say something to you about your own past situation?

JESUS WAS A SINGLE ADULT

A FAMILY MEMBER
Read Luke 2: 41-52; 8: 19-21
How would you describe Jesus' actions/attitude toward his mother in each of these situations?

Read Luke 2: 1-11; John 19: 25-27
In each passage, how did Jesus relate to his mother?
Name the family member(s) you are responsible to help.

Jesus asked a friend (John) to care for his mother after his death. If you are caring for a family member, what person (a relative or friend) can you ask to give you assistance?

List three specific ways in which you need help with your family member.

Can the person you have listed above help you in one of the three ways?

THE LONELY JESUS
Read Matthew 26: 36-45.
What adjectives are used to describe Jesus' emotional condition? (Use a modern translation, such as Phillips.)

Who was with Jesus? What was their relationship to him?

What was Jesus wrestling with in this passage?

Did anyone know the magnitude of his moment of crisis? How did they show it?

Name an area in which you are now struggling.

Is there one person you can name who understands your pain?

What can you learn from this passage that can help you?

LOSING A FRIEND
Read John 11:1-35; Matthew 26:47-50; John 13:36-38, 18:12-27.
How did Jesus lose each of the friends mentioned in the above passages?

Read John 11:36-44; Matthew 27:3-5; John 20:1-9.
What happened to each friend?

Name three friends you have lost and give the reasons why.

Can one of the friendships be recaptured? What steps can you take?

Do you need a *new* friend? Pray about some acquaintances you now have, and ask God to open up a real friendship with one of them for you.

A SEXUAL BEING
Read Luke 8:1-3; 10:39-42; John 11:1-5; John 20.
List some of Jesus' female friends and followers.

Use a concordance and research other passages about them.

How did Jesus relate to them?

What person of the opposite sex can you go to when you want to talk to a male/female friend? (*Not* a dating partner, but a *friend.*)

JESUS WAS A SINGLE ADULT

If you cannot list one here, begin praying that God will surface such a friend of the opposite sex with whom you can relate from time to time.

PURPOSE
Read Luke 4:18.
Use a dictionary to look up the meaning of the following words:

Poor_____   _____
Captive _____   _____
Blind _____   _____
Bruised _____   _____

Do any of the above words relate to someone you know?
Write the person's name beside the word.
What can you do to help that individual?

To whom can you be God's instrument of healing?

Jesus was a single adult who had purpose to his life. What about you?
Continue to look through the Gospels to find out how Jesus Christ related to himself, his followers, his acquaintances, and his father. Discover how he lived as a single adult.

SOME SINGLES' NEEDS

The following is a list of needs most singles (especially the formerly married) find themselves facing at one time or another in their single walk. Some needs have to be dealt with again and again; others need to be faced only once. The reader may enlarge this list as a result of his/her own experience. It is offered here as a starting point for those interested in starting an effort to meet the needs of singles.

• *Loneliness*—How to recognize the difference between being alone and being lonely. How *not* to be encompassed by loneliness. How to take steps to combat it. How to enjoy it. How to realize this feeling is not unique to the single.

• *Self-image*—How to improve a self-image and to project that image to others. Shedding the "loser" image.

• *Leaving the past behind*—A bitterly hurt person finds it difficult *not* to dredge up the past with a lot of "if only . . ." thoughts. "If only we had moved . . . If only I had listened . . . If only he would have . . ." There is a time to move on. How do you leave the past behind?

• *Beginning again*—Life is a shambles for the single just coming through the experience of losing a partner through death or divorce. How do you start putting the pieces back together? Can you? If not, how do you begin again?

• *Trust*—It is hard to trust another human being. Sometimes it is hard to trust God when you have suffered deep hurts. Spiritually, how can you put into practice the verse written years ago:

> Trust him when dark deeds assail thee,
> Trust him when thy needs are small.
> Trust him when to simply trust him
> Seems the hardest thing of all.

Emotionally, how can you begin to trust other people? Is it possible ever to be vulnerable again?

- *Finances*—How do you cope with seeing your financial situation in crisis, making it necessary to drop down two or three levels after divorce? How do you meet daily needs? What about the future?

- *Sexuality*—Physical needs are still there. So are the thoughts. What do I do with them when I am alone?

- *Single Parents*—My children are going through a turmoil of their own, completely separate from mine. How much do they blame me (if separated or divorced)? How can I help heal their hurt? Should I expect them to understand mine? How much should I tell them of my own feelings? How can I help when they tell me theirs?

- *Fun*—Where can I have some? I need to laugh, to talk about light things as well as heavy things. Is there the opportunity? Where? When?

- *Getting things in control*—Taking the initiative to knock anger/hate/bitterness out of my life, rather than letting these emotions control me.

- *Security*—Where is my security in life? In marriage? A partner? Or is there something (or Someone) else to look for security?

- *New experiences*—A single life-style *can* be positive. What new experience will enrich my life?

- *What does Jesus want with me?* Who is Christ? What does he want from my life . . . what does he want to bring to it? Should I view my singleness as something related to him or not? Am I "set apart"? If so, why?